Church Festival Decorations.

SUGGESTION FOR ONE OF A SERIES OF ANGELS RINGING
CHRISTMAS BELLS.

For the decoration of Gallery Fronts, as described on page 71.

Church Festival Decorations:

Being full Directions for

GARNISHING CHURCHES

FOR

And Notes on
OTHER FEASTS
or
FESTIVALS.

CHRISTMAS,
EASTER,
WHITSUNTIDE

AND

HARVEST.

Second Edition, Re-written and Enlarged

BY

ERNEST R. SUFFLING,

Author of "A Treatise on Stained Glass," "Glass Painting for Amateurs," &c.

WITH 97 ILLUSTRATIONS.

LONDON:
L. UPCOTT GILL, BAZAAR BUILDINGS, DRURY LANE, W.C.
NEW YORK:
CHARLES SCRIBNER'S SONS, 153-157, FIFTH AVENUE.
1907.
Republished by Gale Research Company, Book Tower, Detroit, 1974

Library of Congress Cataloging in Publication Data

Suffling, Ernest Richard.
    Church festival decorations.

    1. Flower arrangement in churches. I. Title.
SB449.5.C4S93   1974   745.92'6   74-6266
ISBN 0-8103-4015-1

PREFACE TO THE SECOND EDITION.

During the past two decades Church Festival Decoration has advanced to such an extent that it has now become quite a recognised art. Whereas formerly the display of a few boughs, twigs, and flowers gathered from woods, hedgerows, and gardens was thought sufficient for the purpose of expressing praise and thanks through the medium of decoration, the scheme of garnishing our Churches and Chapels is now regarded as almost an integral part of the Great Festival services, and the whole world is scoured to provide suitable material. Strangely enough, the literature appertaining to the subject is of the most meagre description; hence the entire re-writing of this little book, which it is hoped will, with its many specially prepared illustrations, prove of great assistance to those engaged in either the temporary or the permanent garnishing of our places of worship.

E. R. S.

ERRATA.

p. 23, line 15, *vincit* should be *vinces*.
p. 99, line 15, *exactly* should be *scarcely*.

Church Festival Decorations.

INTRODUCTION.

THE custom of decorating temples probably had its inception many centuries before the coming of Christ, as we know the Romans and Greeks made offerings of fruits and flowers, which were lavishly displayed in the temples of their mythical gods and goddesses. But before those days, the Temple of the Bible, built by Solomon, was on certain occasions decorated in a similar manner.

Records show that flowers formed part of the worship of the divinities of the Assyrians, Babylonians, and even of that still older race, the Egyptians; and if they used the fairest flowers and fruits as humble emblems of the love they bore their false gods, how much more gladly should we make our floral offerings, our cereal offerings, and our offerings of fruit as an acknowledgment of the true God who created both us and them. It is a custom not only sanctioned by our Church, but also having the approval of the Bible itself : " Honour the Lord with thy . . . first fruits . . . so shall thy barns be filled with plenty " (Prov. III. 9, 10 ; see also Lev. XXIII. 40) ; and many other texts on this subject might be quoted, but such a course would be superfluous.

Through the dark ages that succeeded the early days of

B

Christianity the custom has come down with varying rites, and so through the pre-Reformation times to the nineteenth century, when church decoration languished greatly, the custom being carried out in a very perfunctory manner by placing a few sprigs of holly on the tall pew-backs, and strewing about in salient places a few branches of yew or fir, with sprays of ivy or oak. Then came the days when Harvest Frolics usurped the glad usages of the Church, and what were frequently little better than drunken orgies were substituted for praise and prayer for God's bounty.

The early years of the twentieth century give us a far brighter and happier state of things, for whilst Harvest Homes or Frolics are practically dead, church decoration has revived, and has again become a living observance among us, giving congenial work and gladness to thousands, and making God's House the House Beautiful.

On searching into churchwardens' accounts, both before and since the Reformation, we find that it was only at the beginning of last century that the custom fell into abeyance. It is curious to look at the old archives and observe their dates, as they prove that not only at Christmas, but on Palm Sunday, Easter Day, Whitsuntide, Trinity Sunday, and at Harvest, did our ancestors decorate, but that they also continued the practice during the troublous times of the Commonwealth, when nearly every other ceremonial of the Reformed Church was in abeyance.

From contemporary poets we get a proof of the customs in their day. For example, Spenser, the Elizabethan poet, in his " Shepherd's Calendar," which appeared in 1579, says:

> Youths folke now flocken in everywhere
> To gather May buskets* and smeling breere,
> And home they hasten the posts to dight ;
> And all the Kirke pillars ere daylight,
> With Hawthorne buds and sweet Eglantine,
> And Girlonds of Roses——.

---

* Bouquets we now call them.

Here we have the church pillars decked, or dight, with white-thorn, eglantine, sweet briar, and garlands of roses.

Stow, in his " Survey of London," which appeared in 1598, says : " Against the feast of Christmas every 'man's house, as also their Parish Churches, were dressed with holme,* ivy, bayes, and whatever the season of the year afforded to be green."

Here are some items from churchwardens' "accompts" :—
" St Lawrence, Reading, 1505.—It payed to Makrell for the holmebush agayn Christmas ijd." " Parish of St. Mary-at-Hill in ye Citye of London.—Holme and Ivy at Christmas Eve iiijd." " Parish of St. Margaret, Westminster, 1647. —Item, payd for rosemarie and bayes that was stuck about the Church at Christmas, 1s. 6d." In the account for St. Mary's Church, Outwich, London, 1510-11, is this item : " First paid for Palme, box, floures, and cakes iiijd." In the account for All Hallows Staining, London ; " Item, for box and palme on Palme Sunday ; item, for gcnneporet for the Church, ijd." Touching on Easter is an entry in the churchwardens' accounts for St. Mary-at-Hill, London : " Three great garlands for the crosses of roses and lavender, three dozen other garlands for the quire, 3s." Another in St. Martin's Church, Outwich, London, 1525 : " Paid for brome ageynst Easter, jd."

To show that even Puritanical restrictions did not kill the custom, we read in Cole's " Art of Simpling," 1656 : " In some places, setting up of holly, ivy, rosemary, bayes, yew, etc., in Churches at Christmas is still in use." So we might quote many pages to prove that no particular party, High or Low, instituted church decorations in the past century—they simply revived a well-recognised and ancient custom.

The items quoted above furnish us with quite a list of flowers and shrubs used from three to four centuries ago, and they may stand us in good stead for our present-day

---

* The evergreen oak.　† Juniper.

decorations. We have holly, bays, eglantine, broom, roses,
lavender, palms, hawthorn (may or whitethorn), ivy, yew,
box, juniper (gennepore), and if we add a couplet from Gay's
" Trivia," written in 1712, we get two more :

> Now with bright holly all the temples strow,
> With laurel green and sacred mistletoe.

As to the theory of decoration, it should be borne in mind
that whilst the introduction of symbols, monograms, and
other sacred emblems into *temporary decorations* is purely
modern, yet nearly all the devices so used have been in
vogue since the early days of the Christian Church.

This peculiarity regarding the symbols and devices used
should prevent the creeping in of modern innovations not
sanctioned by the Church, and necessitates any worker who
may take the responsibility of the decoration of a church
learning something about the emblems in use, so that their
appropriateness may not be lost by exhibiting devices meant
for a certain festival at a wrong time, whereby the symbolism
is destroyed.

In arranging the decorations, care should be taken
that they enhance, and not detract from, the finer features
of the permanent work of the church, such as the rich
carvings of chancel-screen, pulpit, font, or other fittings.
Where there are dark masses of colour, plain pillars,
straight and uncarved screen mullions, broad window ledges,
and flat or unsightly woodwork or walls, there can the
decorations be placed with positive benefit to the interior,
and without any attempt to " gild the lily " by covering
up and hiding beneath masses of dark foliage the beauties
which left the artificers' hands perhaps centuries ago, when
architectural art was at its zenith.

The true spirit of decoration is to subordinate the love of
mere display to the artistic requirements of the structure; to
bring out its beauties, to conceal its defects, to use only
such symbols as are appropriate to the season, and from year

to year to vary these as much as possible; to brighten the
church with colour neatly arranged without mistaking garish-
ness for joyful brightness. While thus really embellishing
the House of God, the durability and beauty of the permanent fitting must be remembered, and in the eagerness to
put up wreaths and ornaments the stonework of the font
and other parts must not be chipped or stained, nor the fine
woodwork of the various fittings of the church spoilt by
hammering in tacks or nails, or by the application of glue or
other adhesive. The disregard of these important matters
has very rightly caused the vicar and churchwardens of
some churches to forbid decorations of a temporary nature
altogether, for fear the permanent decorations may be spoiled
by irresponsible helpers.

To carry out decoration properly, *system* must be adopted,
and the workers should in all cases be under someone who
will be responsible for the work, and see that no damage is
caused.

Where the proposed decorations are of any considerable
extent, a committee should be formed, including the vicar
and churchwardens, and a plan of the operations formulated,
as a whole. Individuals may then be placed over little
bands of willing workers to carry out the decoration of the
different portions of the church in detail. By this means
the entire, or stated portions of the, church will receive due
attention, instead of some parts of the building receiving
so much elaboration that other parts are thereby neglected,
or spoiled by contrast.

Only by such agreement and abnegation will the work
when completed be a "meet and fitting offering to the
Lord." Church decoration is an offering to the glory of
God, and when there is an unusually skilful worker present,
it is much better that he use his talent to the general benefit
of the whole decorative scheme than that he should employ
all his skill upon a single device which shall earn him praise
by contrast with his less gifted fellow-workers.

The general plan of decoration having been settled, the next thing to do, if the church is large and workers are numerous, is to divide the building into various portions, and to set little bands of workers to carry out the details of decorating particular parts, as pulpit, screen, font, choir stalls, window-sills, &c. Each little band should be under the charge of someone who has had previous experience in such matters, and who knows how to use the various materials to the best advantage.

The work of making wreaths, &c., may be given to the unpractised fingers of newcomers, whilst the making-up of the various devices, which demand more skill, must be reserved for the more expert.

It is an excellent plan to collect all the materials into one room (schoolroom or large vestry) or into a convenient part of the church, and to place someone in charge of it ; otherwise much confusion will arise, and the best of the material will be used for minor decorations, leaving a chaos of débris for other and more important work.

Evergreens.

The following is a list of the principal evergreens :—

Holly, in many varieties.	Arbutus.
Fir, in several varieties.	Privet.
Box, large and small leaved.	Evergreen oak.
Ivy, in several varieties.	Houseleek.
Laurel, do.	Laurustinus.
Arbor vitæ.	Ferns.
Myrtle.	Bay.
Cypress.	Rosemary.
Yew.	Moss and lichen.
Portugal laurel.	

When the evergreens arrive they are usually mingled in much disorder, and some of the gentlemen should at once

separate the different species into heaps, making piles of
holly, according to its various kinds, laurels, fir, yew, evergreen oak, ivy, box, arbor vitæ, privet, laurustinus, and whatever may be sent by friends. Some of the workers may then
go over the various heaps to separate the berried branches of
holly from those which are berryless, and to cut the boughs
into sprays that will be useable in wreaths, &c., rejecting
the thick stems, naked branches, and useless pieces, which
may be thrown into a general refuse heap, handy for clearing
away.

All detached leaves of any kind of evergreen should be
collected, as they come in capitally for forming letters,
borders, and other devices.

Materials for Wreaths, Devices, &c.

Besides the evergreens, many other materials will be required to complete the decorating. Here are some of
them :

Everlasting flowers, coloured and plain.
Imitation holly and ivy berries.
Linen line for foundation of wreaths, &c.
Twine, both thick and thin.
Iron wire for foundations, instead of rope.
Ditto, for binding on evergreens, fixing, &c.
Perforated zinc from which to cut emblems.
Reel wire, as used by florists for flower work.
Deal laths, or plasterers' laths used by builders.
Zinc tubes to hold water for flowers.
Scissors, hammer, pliers for cutting wire.
Fine pointed nails, tacks, paste, gum or glue, &c.

These are the chief requirements for evergreen work; but
when banners, shields, sacred devices, long texts, floral
decorations, &c., are called for, quite a different set of
materials will be in demand, most of which may be

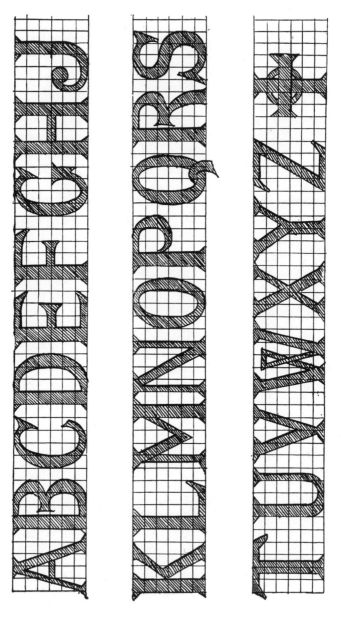

Fig. 1.—ALPHABET OF ROMAN CAPITAL LETTERS set out on Background of Squares to show Mode of Forming the Letters with proportionate Members.

Introduction.

purchased in the nearest town. Here is a list of some of the most useful and necessary articles :

Prepared cloth of various colours.
Red and white twill.
Cotton wool in sheets.
Coloured wall papers.
Flock ditto.
Gold and silver paper.
Cartoon paper (continuous).
Lining ditto.
Prepared cálico.
Straw tissue.

Straw plait.
Oil paints in tubes.
Powdered colours.
Size and whiting.
Gold leaf or gold paint.
Bronze powder.
Japanners' gold size.
Damp-proof paper.
Zinc, both plain and perforated.
Millboard, stout and thin.

Straightedge, square, compasses, pencils, chalk line, &c.

The above is a very fair general list, but where the decoration of a church becomes a fine art, and money is no consideration, there are many other items which might find a place on the list of materials useful for the backgrounds of lettering, for forming devices, &c., some of which are as follow :

American cloth, either coloured, silver, or gold.
Linoleum, upon which to paint large devices, scrolls, &c.
Coloured unglazed cotton.
Ditto, glazed.
White linen swansdown which is plain on one side and fluffy on the other (makes a splendid background for texts, but is expensive).
Scarlet and blue cloths.
Red flannel or flannelette.
Cotton backed velvet, stamped velvets (for banners), &c.

Of course the list might be prolonged to an alarming length, but as a rule the simpler and less costly materials are all that are really necessary.

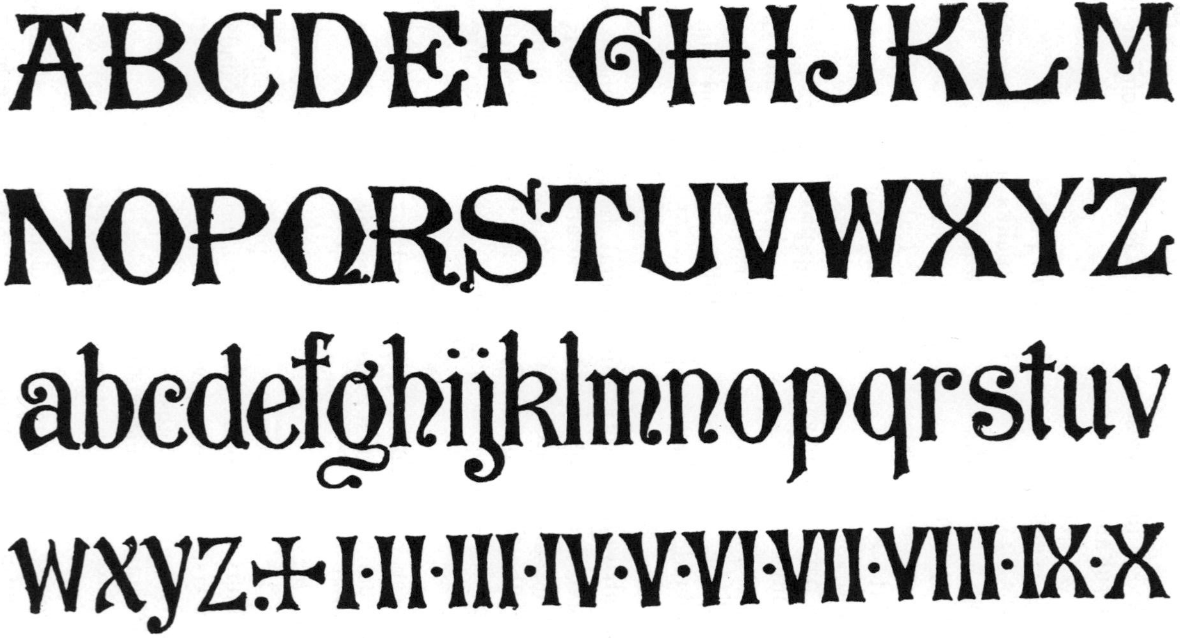

ABCDEFGHIJKLM
NOPQRSTUVWXYZ
abcdefghijklmnopqrstuv
wxyz.✠ I·II·III·IV·V·VI·VII·VIII·IX·X·

Fig. 2.—GOTHIC STYLE OF LETTERING, distinct and without flourishes—Capitals, Small Letters, and Roman Numerals.

Introduction.

It is a fact that in many churches the cost of the *temporary* decorations for three or four years would suffice to decorate the church in a *permanent* and handsome manner.

Almost anything appertaining to church decoration may be had of Messrs. Golding and Plummer, 6 and 7, Little White Lion Street, Shaftesbury Avenue, London.

Lettering for Texts.

As texts are required for each season of the year, and not peculiar to any one in particular, we give here examples of suitable lettering, so that they may be compared. Fig. 1 (page 8) shows the simple Roman letters, and how they may be set out in squares so that they are properly proportioned. Fig. 2 (page 10) illustrates a Gothic style a little more elaborate in its form. Fig. 3 is a modified style of " Church text," which makes a very effective and neat kind of lettering, sufficiently ornamental to have an artistic appearance, and yet not so elaborate as to appear confused when seen at a distance. It may be used for illuminating, but for this purpose another and more suitable example is given at Fig. 4 (page 14). The making and uses of texts will be dealt with in detail under the various festivals.

Emblems.

AGNUS DEI (*the Lamb of God.*)—By this name the Redeemer is frequently described both in the Old and New Testaments. The Lamb was adopted in the earliest ages of Christianity as a type of our Lord. The oldest examples show the lamb standing upon a mound from which flow four rivers. The Lamb of God always has the Divine nimbus and sometimes carries the Flag of Resurrection.

ALPHA AND OMEGA (A and Ω).—The first and last letters of the Greek alphabet, typical of our Lord and suitable for all festivals.

ANCHOR.—Signifies Hope, or Patience, or with a cross beam Faith. A *Heart* is emblematic of Charity or Love.

Fig. 3.—A MODIFIED STYLE OF CHURCH TEXT LETTERING—Capitals, Small Letters, and Figures.

ANIMALS.—The *Lamb* we have previously mentioned under " Agnus Dei " (page 11). The *Lion* typifies strength and vigilance. The *Ox*, the emblem of St. Mark, a sacrifice. The Ass, *patience;* often shown with the ox at our Lord's birth. The *Hart* in early times was emblematic of baptism. The *Horse* sometimes carries a palm branch in its mouth in remembrance of St. Paul in the arena or course. The *Swine*, the emblem of St. Anthony.

ARCHANGELS' EMBLEMS.—These are as follow :

St. Gabriel—Sceptre or lily.

St. Michael—Pair of scales (justice), or a staff surmounted by cross fleury ; a flaming sword.

St. Raphael—Fish or pilgrim's staff.

St. Uriel—Roll or book.

Archangels are represented with coronet and cross on their foreheads, portending their constant war against Satan and his angels.

BANNERS.—The remembrance of the banner carried to victory by Constantine is perpetuated by the ecclesiastic banner depending from a cross-piece. The heraldic banner is affixed to a staff.

BIRDS.—The *Peacock* renewing its feathers was an emblem of the resurrection. The *Eagle*, used as an emblem of our Lord's resurrection ; also the emblem of St. John the Evangelist. The *Dove* is the symbol of the Holy Ghost, but when shown with an olive branch in its mouth it represents peace. The *Raven*, chosen by God to feed the prophet in the wilderness, typifies God's providence. The *Hen and Chickens* indicate the same. The *Pelican*, usually represented feeding its young from its breast, is an emblem of our Lord ; also of piety. The *Phœnix* is an emblem of resurrection. The *Cock*, as announcing the rising of the sun, is used also as an emblem of the resurrection ; it was placed on ancient monuments as an emblem of hope ; sometimes typifies vigilance, and sometimes, as on St. Peter's Day, denotes repentance.

Fig. 4.—EXAMPLES OF LETTERS FOR ILLUMINATING.—The best effects are secured by using only a few colours.

Introduction.

COLOURS.—Although under the various headings colours
will be fully dealt with, it will be well here to give some
preliminary general information, for not only may it
be the means of preventing willing workers from falling into error, but it will give them confidence in what
they do. The five Canonical colours are red, white, violet,
green, and black. White is the most joyous of the colours,
but is sometimes represented by gold.

The great seasons and festivals of the Church have each
their distinctive colours, as follow :

Advent, violet.

Christmas Eve to the Octave of Epiphany, white.

Christmas Day itself is an exception, when the colours are
red, green, and white.

Lent, violet.

Good Friday, black and grey.

Easter to the Vigil of Pentecost, white (gold, blue, and red
are also used in decorations).

Vigil of Pentecost, red.

Whitsuntide, white.

Trinity, red, white, and blue.

Ember weeks (in September), violet.

All Saints' Day, white.

Purification of the Virgin Mary, white.

Annunciation Day, white.

Holy Innocents' Day, if on a Sunday, red ; if on a week-
day, violet.

Septuagesima, Sexagesima, and Quinquagesima Sundays,
violet.

Rogation Days, white.

Public Fasts, black.

Four Evangelists' Days, white.

Saints' days, white (Martyrs' days excepted, when the
colour is red).

The altar cloths, frontals for pulpit, lectern, and reading-
desk should be arranged in the way indicated on the days.

mentioned. As to temporary decorations, such as are dealt with in this book, the colours need not be, and seldom are, so strictly adhered to as in the permanent furnishings of the church.

It may be taken as an axiom that the use of other colours is permissible so long as the predominant colour is the one appropriate to the day, and used, where possible, in the making of the different symbols.

Now a few words as to *the use of colours as seen at a distance*. The power of colours in reflecting light varies considerably, and must be taken into consideration when making devices which are not meant to be viewed close to the eye. The upper atmosphere being more rarefied and less encumbered with vapour than the lower, colours do not disappear so quickly as those placed horizontally with the line of sight. Thus a coloured device placed say twenty-five feet high upon a wall, will be just as plain to the eye as the same device placed upon the same wall five feet from the ground, although it will be some ten feet farther away, supposing the observer to be standing some thirty feet from the wall. To obtain a clear idea of the reflective power of various colours, a good plan is to cut out discs of colour three inches across, to fix them on a wall, to walk about twenty-five feet from them, and then to turn round and scrutinise them.

Yellow, being the colour which reflects most light, is seen more plainly than any other (provided of course that the background is dark). Red, being closely allied to yellow, comes next, and the nearer the red approaches bright orange or vermilion, the more distinct will it appear. *Green* reflects light according to the amount of yellow in its composition, that is to say, the nearer it approaches yellow in tone the farther off it can be distinguished; but the more blue it contains the less light it reflects, and the shorter the distance at which it will be visible. *Blue*, having no yellow in its composition, is not seen to advantage from a distance;

in fact, a full deep blue appears black, but becomes more visible as it has white mixed with it to make it paler. Notice should be taken of blue by daylight, and blue by gas or lamp light. A certain piece of a pale blue material will look several shades darker by artificial light than by daylight, and a dark blue will appear black when viewed by artificial light. Green leaves look very much " bluer " by artificial light than by day, therefore for churches pale or yellow toned evergreens are preferable to dark ones, because, although yellow-toned leaves look bluer at night, yet they are of a pleasant green, whereas blue-green or dark-toned evergreens go black and have a funereal appearance. Yellow by artificial light appears but a cream colour, and deep chrome only an ordinary yellow.

Another thing to be noted is that certain colours change completely when placed in juxtaposition. Try this experiment. Cut off some strips of brightly coloured paper half an inch wide and a foot long, fasten them edge to edge, close together, on a wall, in a good light. First place a strip of yellow and a strip of bright medium blue paper together, walk twenty-five feet away from them, then turn round and notice what has happened. Instead of two strips of paper, one blue and one yellow, each half an inch wide, you will see a single strip of green paper an inch wide. The colours will mingle completely. So with other colours. Some when placed in juxtaposition will keep their places, while others will not. Try them, and note in your pocket-book the effect of the various combinations; you will thus learn an invaluable lesson in decoration.

All combinations of colour are bad reflectors, unless largely composed of yellow. Thus a pale yellow-green is seen at a much greater distance than any other green, and the palest blue keeps its colour distinctly, whereas a dark blue at the same distance becomes black to the eye. Attention to this is very necessary in decorating a chancel which is to be viewed from the nave of the church.

C

CROSSES.—The cross is the first and greatest symbol of Christianity. It has been idealised and given many forms, some of which are never used in church decoration, and, indeed, in heraldry have become much distorted.

The different crosses were divided into classes at the time of the great schism between the Eastern and Western Churches, and for a long period each Church used its particular and distinct kind; the Western Church retaining and using the *Latin Cross*, which is believed to represent the form of the true cross upon which our Saviour died, whilst

Fig. 5.—Cross of Atonement, or Cross of Calvary.

Fig. 6.—Cross of the Resurrection

Fig. 7.—Cross of Iona, or Irish Cross.

the Eastern Church preferred and adopted the *Greek Cross*, a more ideal and decoratively manageable symbol.

Cross Fleury (Fig. 8).—A cross having the ends of the limbs ornamented like flowers—really a fleur-de-lys end to each limb.

Cross of Atonement (Fig. 5).—The same as the Latin Cross, but mounted upon three steps which represent Faith, Hope, and Love (or Charity). Sometimes it is jewelled, when it is known as the *Cross of Glory*. As an Atonement Cross it is used on Christmas Day and at Whitsuntide, as a Passion Cross on Ash Wednesday, and through Lent to Good Friday, on which day all crosses are removed from the church.

Cross of Iona, or *Irish Cross* (Fig. 7).—This is in the shape of the Latin cross, but with the ends of the upper limbs expanded, and has a circle surrounding the axis of the four quarters. It is said to have been the first cross ever used in Great Britain, and is employed by the Irish to the present day. Anciently it stood in nearly every village, either at the crossways, at the roadside, or in the churchyard. Many relics of this type of cross still remain in England.

Cross of the Resurrection (Fig. 6).—A tall slender cross, the lower limb being of unlimited length, while the three upper limbs are of equal length and all terminate in circles or

Fig. 8.—Cross Fleury.   Fig. 9.—Cross Pommée.   Fig. 10.—Cross Urdée.

balls. This cross is used from Easter until Whitsuntide, including Ascension Day.

Cross Pattée.—Similar to the Maltese Cross (Fig. 14).

Cross Pommée (Fig. 9).—A Greek cross with knobs or circles at the end of each limb. It was the armorial ensign of the Crusader Kings of Jerusalem, who bore five golden crosses upon a silver shield—a solitary violation of the heraldic law that "metal cannot be placed upon metal."

Cross Urdée (Fig. 10).—Represents the four nails which pierced our Lord.

Gamma Cross (Fig. 11).—Built up fancifully from four of the Greek letters Γ (gamma).

Greek Cross (Fig. 13).—This has all four limbs of equal length, and is emblematic of the good tidings borne to the four corners of the earth by the four Gospels. It should be

C 2

used at Christmas, Whitsuntide, and Trinity, but in conjunction with and not to the exclusion of the Latin Cross.

Latin Cross (Fig. 12).—This, the true cross, has its three upper arms of equal length, and the lower one indefinitely prolonged. It is also known as the Passion Cross.

Fig. 11.—Gamma Cross.   Fig. 12.—Latin or Passion Cross.   Fig. 13.—Greek Cross.

Maltese Cross (Fig. 14).—This, the badge of the Knights of Malta, belongs to the Eastern type of crosses, and is an equal-armed cross with the outer ends so widely spread as each nearly to touch its neighbour. It is sometimes called the *Eight-Pointed Cross*. The Maltese Cross may be used as secondary to other crosses for any kind of church

Fig. 14.—Maltese Cross, or Cross Pattée.   Fig. 15.—St. Andrew's Cross.   Fig. 16.—Tau or Egyptian Cross.

decoration, except during Lent, but should at no time be placed in any prominent position, and never on the Communion Table.

Passion Cross.—This cross is the Latin Cross, plain, simple, and unadorned in any way. In mediæval times this was known as the *Cross of Shame*.

Introduction.

St. Andrew's Cross (Fig. 15).—This represents the cross upon which the saint is supposed to have suffered martyrdom, in token of his unworthiness, even in death, to imitate the actions of his Divine Master. It is used as a symbol of humility, and therefore has no place in the decorations of Easter, Ascension, or Trinity.

Tau, Potent, Crutch, Jewish, and Egyptian Crosses (Fig. 16).—These are one and the same, being similar in form to the Latin Cross, but with the top member omitted. It is called the Tau Cross because of its resemblance to the Greek letter T = tau. It is only used during the season of Advent, as it represents the cross of the Old Testament, or *Anticipatory Cross*. In ancient Missal paintings this cross is the one always shown when the miracle of the Brazen Serpent is depicted.

CROWNS.—These represent the kingly power and majesty of our Lord. There are also the Crown of Victory, crowns of flowers and starry crowns. The Crown of Thorns is one of the principal emblems of the Passion. The crown is also the emblem of martyrdom.

EVANGELISTS' EMBLEMS.—These are four winged figures, thus :—

St. John—Eagle.
St. Luke—Winged ox.
St. Matthew—Angel.
St. Mark—Winged lion.

All four usually carry inscribed scrolls with the name of the Evangelist, or with the commencing sentence of their Gospels.

FISH.—On account of the Greek word for fish—Iχθυs—comprising the initials of the words Jesus Christ, Son of God, the Saviour, this was taken as a symbol by early Christians. Sometimes the fish is represented alone ; sometimes two are placed one above the other (head to tail), and sometimes three are arranged in the form of a triangle.

FLOWERS are types of God's bounty and of man's praise. The *Lily* is the emblem of purity and innocence, or chastity, and with the fleur-de-lys is assigned to the Virgin Mary. The *Rose* is for love, and when combined with the lily represents the Rose of Sharon and the Lily of the Valley. The *Marigold* and *Daisy* are also dedicated to the Virgin mother. The *Oak leaf* represents strength, virtue, and force; the *Ivy*, always remaining green, everlasting life; the *Palm*, Christian victory; the *Olive*, peace; the *Laurustinus*, immortality; *Laurel*, victory and constancy; *Cypress*, birth, from being planted in Eastern countries when a child is born.

The *Passion Flower* holds a unique position among flowers, being peculiarly typical of our Lord's Passion. Its leaves are considered to represent the shape of the spearhead which pierced our Saviour's side; the five points of the leaves, the five wounds; the tendrils, the cords which bound His wrists, and the whips with which He was beaten; the ten petals, the ten Apostles who witnessed the Crucifixion (Judas being dead, and Peter absent, having denied his Master); the pillar in the centre, the Cross; the stamens, the hammers; the styles, the nails; the inner circle round the pillar, the crown of thorns; and the large number of small petals, forming a circle round the pillar, the nimbus or glory. The white part of the flower is an emblem of purity, and the blue colour of the rest is typical of Heaven.

FRUIT is also considered an emblem of God's bounty. *Grapes* and *Ears of Corn* or a *Maize Cob* symbolise the Sacrament. *Pomegranates* represent royalty (the top being like a crown in form), also the future life. The *Apple* typifies the fall of man; the *Fig*, fruitfulness.

LAMPS.—Symbols of the glory of the Saints. If a lamp is placed in the hand of our Lord it represents Him as the Light of the World. Five lighted and five unlighted lamps represent the Wise and Foolish Virgins, or wisdom and improvidence.

Introduction.

Magi.—For the Epiphany the offerings of the Wise Men, gold, myrrh, and frankincense, are correct symbols. Vases or elaborate little caskets or coffers are the pictorial representations of these gifts. *Gold* signifies the regal power of our Lord; *frankincense* His Godhead; and *myrrh*, His humanity (the latter being used for embalming the dead). Legend relates that the Wise Men were three Eastern kings; hence they are frequently represented by three crowns.

Monograms.—The earliest monogram is that displayed on the Labarum or Banner of Constantine. It consists of the first two Greek letters of our Lord's name: x = chi, p = rho, and is written thus : ☧, or in the form of a cross, thus : ☦. Sometimes the p is placed through an n in this form ☧ when it is read ΧΡΙΣΤΟΣ ΝΙΚΑ (Christ conquers). Sometimes the words " In hoc signo vincit " (in this sign shalt thou conquer) are added.

Musical Instruments.—For gallery-fronts, organ-lofts, &c., these may be made to form centre-pieces surrounded with garlands. They may be painted on linoleum, or modelled in clay, sized and painted. The principal ones mentioned in the Bible are tabret or harp, trumpet, psaltery (lute), pipe, organ, cymbals, cornet (Pan pipes), flute, sackbut, dulcimer, tabor, horn, and sistrum.

Orb and Sceptre.—These are used to symbolise majesty and power.

Passion Emblems.—These are very numerous, and embrace : (1) the cross fleury, emblematic of glory and triumph; (2) five crosses fleury, representing the five wounds, the centre cross being larger than the others; (3) the implements of the Passion : Crown of thorns, dice, nails, hammer, pincers, ladder, spear, sword, reed and sponge, bulrushes, coat without seam, pillow of scourging, scourges, rope, lantern, clubs and staves, thirty pieces of silver, chalice (the agony in Gethsemane), basin and ewer, cock, label inscribed " I.N.R.I.," &c.

SAINTS' EMBLEMS.—These are as follow :—

St. Andrew—Cross saltire.

St. Bartholomew—Flaying knife and skin over arm.

St. David—Leek.

St. George—Red cross on a white shield.

St. James the Great—Pilgrim's staff ; shell, staff, and wallet ; or sword and book.

St. James the Less—Fuller's club.

St. John the Baptist—Lamb and staff, with banner inscribed, " Ecce Agnus Dei " ("Behold the Lamb of God ").

St. John the Evangelist—Chalice, with dragon or eagle ; palm branch ; eagle.

St. Jude—Halbert, carpenter's square, ship.

St. Luke—Winged ox ; also emblems appertaining to painting.

St. Mark—Winged lion.

St. Matthew—Spear, carpenter's square, money-bag, showing his calling (that of a tax gatherer).

St. Matthias—Axe.

St. Nicholas—Child in his arms ; three apples.

St. Patrick—Staff and shamrock.

St. Paul—Sword and book.

St. Peter—Gold and silver keys.

St. Philip—Spear or cross.

St. Simon—Fuller's bat, saw, owl.

St. Stephen—Three stones, palm branch, and crown.

St. Thomas—Dart or javelin.

SWORDS.—When depicted with a sharp or acute point, the sword is known as the *Sword of Justice;* when with an obtuse or blunt point, the *Sword of Religion;* and when with a square end and a blunt edge, the *Sword of Mercy.* A sword surrounded by flames typifies Divine vengeance.

Besides the lists of emblems given above, there are others which may be used, but are not often seen. They are as follow :

Ark represents God's promise : the Church.

Censer represents prayer.

Crystal represents purity and innocence.

Emerald represents unfading youth ; eternity.

Five-Pointed Star represents the Star of Bethlehem.

Flaming Heart represents the love of God.

Flaming Sword represents the wrath of God.

Heptagon, or Septfoil, represents the gifts of the Holy Ghost ; the Creation.

Hexagon, or Sexfoil, represents the six great attributes of God—glory, honour, majesty, omnipotence, power, and wisdom.

Lion (without wings) represents Our Lord ; the Lion of Judah.

Moon represents the Virgin Mary ; helpfulness.

Nine-Pointed Star represents the Holy Ghost.

Pentagon represents the five wounds.

Ruby represents Divine love.

Sapphire represents celestial contemplation.

Sceptre represents an archangel.

Seven-Pointed Star represents perfection.

Ship represents the Church.

Six-Pointed Star represents Creation.

Square represents the Holy City.

Sun represents God's light ; the Creation.

Trefoil represents the Trinity.

Triangle represents the Trinity.

Trumpet represents the voice of God.

Dried Flowers, Grasses, Palms, &c.

As many products of distant lands are now available in a dried state for purposes of decoration, it will be worth while to say a few words concerning them, and give the prices at which they can usually be purchased. The latter are necessary, as church folk are frequently charged absurdly high prices in country villages for what may be obtained for a small sum in town.

ASPARAGUS (*plumosus nanus*) and SMILAX.—These may be used either in the natural state or dried.

BULRUSHES may be had in many parts of England for the mere gathering, but cost from 9d. to 1s. 6d. per dozen to buy.

EVERLASTING FLOWERS.—*Cape Flowers.*—A large kind of everlasting flower, almost pure white, and found only in the neighbourhood of Cape Town. Price (natural),

Fig. 17.—Everlasting Flowers (Helichrysums).

1s. 6d. per hundred, opened and wired, ready for use; coloured ones 3d. per hundred extra.

Fairy Flowers.—These are a variety of thistle, white, and of a beautiful, pure, silky texture. Price 15s. per 100; coloured 18s.

Helichrysums (Fig. 17.)—The natural colours of these flowers range from pure white to crimson.

In country places, where nearly everyone has a garden of some kind, it will be found much less expensive to grow than to buy Helichrysums. They bloom very freely for quite three months. The full blooms should be taken off during fine, dry days, and not allowed to remain upon the plants after they are fully developed, or their petals will become loose, and they will prevent other flowers from forming. When gathered they should be well dried in the sun or near a fire and stored away in an insect-proof box in a dry place. A piece of naphthalene placed with the flowers will help to protect them from insects.

The daughters of the villagers or farmers will often gladly undertake this task, and will then naturally take more

Fig. 18.—Immortelles (Gnaphaliums).

interest in the church and its adornment; moreover, by this means friendly relations are often established between the cottage and the vicarage.

Immortelles (*Gnaphaliums*, Fig. 18).—These are more used in church decorations than any other flower, and are sold tied in large bundles at 1s. or 1s. 3d. each, or at about 12s. per dozen. They are all ready for the workers' hands, and may be had in numerous colours—yellow, white, blue, scarlet, violet, maroon, &c.

Acrocliniums and Rhodanthes are other useful varieties of everlasting flowers.

FERNS, &c.—Maidenhair (*Adianthum cuneatum*), 1s. to

1s. 6d. per dozen. Resurrection Fern (*Selaginella brasiliensis*), dried and preserved, 1s. bundle.

GRASSES.—*Bromus brizæformis.*—A fine bushy plant filled with little seed heads. Should be used with its dried lily-like leaves. Comes from Germany, and may be had natural or artificially coloured at 1s. 9d. per lb.

Brown African Grasses.—Long-stemmed and in much variety. 2s. per lb.

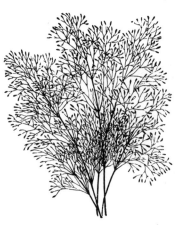

Fig. 19.—Cloud Grass (Agrostis nebulosa).

Fig. 20.—Hair Grass (Aira pulchella).

Cloud Grass (Agrostis nebulosa, Fig. 19).—A fine decorative grass for work to be viewed near, but too shadowy for bold devices. A native of the South of France, Algeria, and Italy. 6d. per bunch, or 4s. per dozen.

English Reed Grass (Stipa lasiagrostis).—May be had all over England for a few pence.

Feather Grass (Stipa pennata).—As its name implies, a tall feather-like grass; native of Austria. May be had: white at 3s. per dozen bunches; coloured 4s. 6d. per dozen.

Hair Grass (Aira pulchella, Fig. 20).—A similar grass to, and may be mixed with, the above. 6d. per bunch, or 4s. per dozen.

Introduction.

Hare's-tail Grass (Lagurus ovatus).—A very pretty plant with tall spiky seed pods.

Pampas Grass (Gynerium argenteum.)—From California and South America. Runs (in a dried state) from 2ft. or less up to 3½ft. high, and costs from 2s. to 4s. per dozen, or a little more when dyed.

Trembling or Quaking Grasses (Briza maxima and *minor).* —Very similar to *Bromus,* and about the same price. Come chiefly from Spain.

Uva Grass (Gynerium saccharoides).—This is a splendidly decorative grass, running from 4ft. to 7ft. high, greyish white in colour, and with long soft foliage on one side only ; a native of the Brazilian jungles. The price ranges, according to length, from 3s. to 6s. per dozen ; coloured from 5s. to 10s. per dozen.

PALMS.—*Areca lutescens* leaves are feathery, with large spaces between the leaflets, and from 15in. to 40in. high. Prices range from 1s. 6d. to 5s. per dozen for the naturally dried branches, but from 3s. to 15s. if coloured green.

Cycas revoluta.—These leaves might be mistaken for gigantic feathers of various colour, being very regular in form and having a quill-like stem showing up the centre. They may be had from 1ft. to 3½ft. high, already dyed, at from 3s. to 7s. per dozen.

Kentia Leaves, from Lord Howe's Island in the Pacific Ocean, are of very beautiful form and suitable for bold decoration ; they are from 1ft. to 3ft. high, and range in price from 4s. 6d. the small to 10s. 6d. for the large size. Cheaper leaves of the same style, but not so handsome, are those of *Areca lutescens.*

Latania borbonica.—Lovely fan-like leaves, broader than high. They make a splendid background for a floral or other device, measuring from 2½ft. to 4ft. across. Average cost 1s. each.

Phœnix Leaves or *Jerusalem Palms.*—These are imported direct from the Holy Land, and, unlike the Uva grass, are furnished with leaflets on both sides. They make a magnificent decoration, running from 4ft. to 7ft. in length, and cost from 3s. 6d. to 5s. per dozen as imported, or a little more if unopened and prepared. Picked specimens of these leaves may be had just before Palm Sunday, standing from 9ft. to 10ft. high, and costing from 3s. to 4s. 6d. each.

Sabal Leaves.—Rounded leaves, copiously divided. From 2s. 6d. to 4s. per dozen.

Most of the above leaves and plants may be purchased made up into " palms," which, when placed in cork or other artistic pots, have a very natural and decorative appearance. Many varieties are available, and any leading artificial florist will send a list upon application.

Dried Mosses.

These are an important feature in all church devices, and often get one over a difficulty in background colouring when nothing else appears to be suited for the purpose; indeed, moss seems to stand alone in its usefulness as a decorating medium. It is good for letters, for borders, for backgrounds, and as a screen to hide ugly pots and ugly nooks in architecture.

In country places, the natural, growing moss with its beautiful colouring may be had for the gathering; but where it is not to be so easily obtained, it must be purchased from the artificial florist.

FRENCH Moss.—This may be had of a dark or light green colour, and is tied in bunches which cost about 3s. per dozen; but when large quantities are required it is cheaper to buy it by the case of 240 bunches, for 45s. It will keep if not required for present work. If the purchaser is content to have the moss in its natural colour, it comes much less expensive—2s. 6d. per dozen bunches, or 20s. per crate.

RESURRECTION Moss.—A very pretty fern-like moss, which will keep fresh and green for years. It costs 4s. per dozen bunches.

SIBERIAN MOSS.—This, of a beautiful silver grey colour, is the kind florists use for making their wreaths and devices (anchors, crowns, &c.), and is therefore very appropriate for church decoration. Before using, it must be soaked for half an hour in a pail of water in which a handful of ordinary table salt has been well stirred. When thoroughly saturated, the moss should be taken out and squeezed, when it will be ready for use. It has the faculty of keeping moist for an indefinite period. Sold in wooden boxes at 1s. 3d. each, or 12s. per dozen.

To the above lists may be added home dried and pressed ferns, flowers, and beautiful leaves of many kinds, so dried that they retain their natural colours, and are available for decorative purposes at all seasons of the year.

All kinds of dried palms, grasses and flowers, also artificial flowers, may be purchased at Messrs. Hartung and Puetz's establishment, 65, Long Acre, London.

Adhesives.

Among church decorators there is a great diversity of opinion as to the best adhesive to use, and many nostrums—some rather expensive—have been put on the market.

Ordinary glue well thinned out is very good, but it must always be kept hot, which is a nuisance when it is wanted in half-a-dozen places in the church at the same time. *Liquid Glue* is another form, but does not require heating. *Gum Arabic* dissolved in cold water is very clean, but must be used very thick to be of service. It must be stirred frequently for a couple of days before it is thoroughly melted. It may be made with hot water, but does not then keep nearly so long. *Gum Tragacanth* is sometimes used for delicate work, such as frosting letters or fixing rice. *Isinglass* melted in hot water is also used for the same and similar purposes, but as an adhesive gum is very weak and not adapted for fastening anything but the tiniest object. *Strong Paste*, which will be found efficient for most purposes,

may be prepared as follows :—Take a breakfast-cupful of
flour and put it in a basin with a little *cold* water ; mix
it to a very smooth paste and stand aside. Next powder
some alum—a piece about the size of a small walnut—and
also melt a piece of glue about the same size in boiling water,
and put aside also.   Upon the flour paste pour *boiling* water
and stir with a large wooden spoon until it " turns," that is,
forms a semi-transparent paste.   Place paste, alum, and glue
into a saucepan and boil for two or three minutes, and the
result will be an unusually strong paste which will fasten
practically anything.

Christmas.

We will commence our practical instructions on church decorations with the first great festival of the Church year, Christmas, although to some laymen it may appear that Easter should have first place. As much of the advice given under this heading applies equally to the other seasons of the Church, the reader will do well to peruse this portion with care, as the information is not repeated under the headings of other festivals.

The decoration of our places of worship, both churches and chapels, at Christmas, has now become so general that for one of them to be seen ungarnished at that festival is a great rarity. There are some of us who can remember the time when the style of symbolising our Saviour's birth was a single branch of holly stuck upright on every pew and upon the pulpit, which transformed the interior of the church into a miniature forest for a period of six weeks. Sometimes, where holly was plentiful, branches would also be stood in the window recesses, thus ensuring a dismal light to the interior during dull days. This is now, happily, altered, and the question of how a church is to be decorated so as to display the workers' artistic taste, and yet not to mar the architectural beauty of the building, is one of interest to us all. Whereas in past days indigenous evergreens formed the sum-total of decorative materials, we now ransack the whole

D

world, for our grasses, flowers, and palms, our fruits and mosses, and a great number of other materials are utilised.

Wreaths.

In most books it is emphatically laid down that wreaths in festoons are to be deprecated in church decorations—that the straight lines of the architecture, etc., should be adhered to. Such rules to some may appear correct; but surely there is another side to the question, as, after all, the temporary decorations form not an integral part of the building, but an addition to it. It is a canon of Art that straight lines are less elegant than curves, and it is recognised that diversity and beauty are secured by placing a curve to oppose a straight line, and a straight line to break or support a curve. Why, then, ornament a straight line by superimposing another straight line of decoration upon it? There is, perhaps, a formal, if monotonous, beauty in straight-sided figures; but have not curves a still greater claim to beauty? If not, why have we the graceful curves in the tracery pieces of our church windows, the beautiful roundness of our clustered columns, and the exquisite curves and scrolls of the capitals? Surely the natural beauties of the fabric of the church are strong enough to stand alone without incurring a risk of being marred because they are garnished with a few curves, spirals, or festoons of evergreens?

Most writers say decorate sparingly: then, for that reason, curves should not be deleted from the general scheme, for one curved wreath will be as effective as two placed in stiff, straight lines. Probably a happy compromise may settle the question by a little taste being displayed in so arranging curved decorations that they do not spoil the repose of the general lines of the object they are meant temporarily to beautify. Architecture and decoration should go hand-in-hand, but if in their zeal a little band of workers should, with a few green leaves, transgress the standing rules of architecture in a transient manner, the peccadillo dies with the removal of their

handiwork. Not every village lad or lass is a Wren or an
Inigo Jones.

The best foundation for long evergreen wreaths is thin
rope or clothes line, which may be had at about a penny for
three yards, and is best bought in balls when a large quantity
is required. It will be found the best plan to cut off the
rope to the length required *before* attaching the evergreens.

By suspending the rope taut between any available holds,
pew-ends, pillars, or other objects, so that it is about three
feet from the ground, the workers can get at it well for
fastening on the evergreens. Whilst this is being done,
others may be doing the same with long deal laths, which
should first be cut to fit the places for which they are meant.

For the laths somewhat finer material may be used than
for the ropes. Good pieces of arbor vitæ, box, evergreen
oak, ivy, yew, and unberried holly should be placed on them
and bound in position by fine wire. The advantage of
placing the evergreens systematically upon the laths is at
once apparent when finished, as it gives them a clear and
distinct appearance, and separates such work entirely from
the rougher wreaths.

As the laths are covered they may be handed to another
worker to finish by adding little bunches of real or artificial
holly berries at regular intervals, binding them in position
with thin iron wire. If these lath wreaths and rope wreaths
are placed along the front of a gallery the smaller or lath
wreaths should go along the top, and the thicker rope
wreaths at the bottom, being broader and fuller.

The rope wreaths may in most cases be made of larger and
rougher materials than those placed on the laths. Holly,
ivy, laurels, and other large leaves are suitable for the
purpose. It has a good effect where a wreath is placed over
the chancel arch to allow long tendrils of ivy to depend from
it. These should be fixed to the main rope before it is put
in position, and when it is hung, should any of the tendrils
not hang gracefully, or not be required, they may be cut off

with a pair of scissors by a man mounted on a ladder. This stalactite kind of wreath also looks well over windows.

In no case should the wreaths be made too thick or full, or they will lose their grace and appear cumbersome, massive, and ineffective. A wreath or garland should be proportionately stout to its length, letting it be rather slim than obese. There is more grace in a single tendril of ivy than in a whole untied faggot of evergreen. Besides which, wagon loads of evergreen foliage have a decidedly sickly odour in a church, especially when the building has to be kept closed during the cold days.

It gives an overburdened appearance to wind thick wreaths around slender objects, such as Communion rails, screen mullions, or the supports of the reading desk or pulpit ; these should be ornamented with thin wreaths of selected small leaves bound on stout twine.

The Pillars.

When the pillars of the nave are plain, they should be decorated with either a narrow wreath made like those described for the galleries, only on fine rope, arranged spirally round them, and the capitals adorned with the same kind of wreath, but having variegated holly, ivy, and plenty of berries on it ; or by three bands of red cloth about eight inches wide being placed at equal distances round them, and narrow wreaths of holly, evergreen oak, fir, box, laurustinus, unberried holly, or other evergreen placed upon the red cloth ; each wreath to be composed of only one kind of evergreen. The three wreaths on each pillar may be of the same foliage, but each pillar, if possible, may be adorned with a different shrub. No flower or berry of any sort need be used, as the necessary colour is already obtained by the red cloth. The edges of the cloth may be scalloped or vandyked.

The capital of the pillar may be decorated thus : Take three large dark ivy leaves and sew them upon a piece of cardboard, which should be thin, one upright and the other two horizontally. Where the three stalks meet put a bunch of holly berries. Alternate these with round bosses made of dark holly or bunches of ivy berries, and place 6in. apart round the capital or just beneath it.

Should the columns not be plain but fluted, or in clusters of pillars, sew on, one by one, holly leaves upon a base of green tape, and place them up the flutes or hollows as a wreath.

Another plan is to cut off deal laths a trifle longer than the height of the columns, so that they will spring into place without any nails or wires being used. The laths should first be painted green or red, and holly, oak, or laurel leaves tacked on, each overlapping the one above it slightly. If the deal laths are painted red, little pieces may be allowed to peep out here and there with good effect and to the saving of berries. Ivy sprays, hanging with short tendrils, have a good effect when merely twined round the columns in a spiral form.

Thin wreaths looped in tiny festoons round the capitals look well, especially if each junction is set off with a few berries or coloured everlasting flowers, or Cape flowers.

Of course, the use of red cloth, linen, or flannel must greatly depend upon whether the interior of the church is of brick, stone, or wood, and the degree of light in it; but it should be freely used except where red brick has to be decorated.

Red, green, and white are the correct ecclesiastic colours for Christmas : red as the symbol of Divine Love and Creative Power, white as the symbol of Innocence, Faith, Joy, and Regeneration, and green signifying the Bounty of God.

Further suggestions for decorating pillars will be found in Figs. 52 to 55, pages 76 to 78.

Emblems and Devices.

Having finished the rougher work of wreath making, the

finer decorations, such as emblems, texts, &c., may be taken in hand, all of which should typify in some manner the birth and mission of our Saviour and His divine attributes.

The window-sills of a church, being generally wide and deep, afford good space for the display of emblems, texts, &c. As a rule, to prevent soiling or staining by damp, a foundation is cut to the splayed shape to prevent damage, and to act as a background for the devices or texts.

For this purpose damp-proof paper, zinc (permanent though more expensive), or thin wood may be chosen.

Fig. 21.—The Double Triangle— Emblem of the Trinity.

Fig. 22.—The Shield of Faith, surrounded by a Circle symbolising Eternity.

Instead of covering the entire sill with thin deal boards, frames of deal, an inch thick and 3in. wide, may be made, the ends being " halved " together and fastened with brass screws, which will not rust. These should be covered with waterproof paper, which may be bought in twelve-yard rolls.

We will now give a few outline drawings of shapes of emblems for covering with evergreens or other materials. Fig. 21 is the double triangle, emblem of the *Trinity*. It may be cut from zinc or stout millboard, or made with deal laths fastened with small screws at the angles and also where the strips cross each other. There are many modes of decorating the triangles; one is to cover one triangle with red berries, and the other with evergreen leaves.

Another plan is to use yellow-green leaves on one and dark blue-green leaves on the other; golden holly or arbor vitæ leaves for the former, and ivy or box for the latter. Small leaves should be selected.

When the foundation is of wood or millboard, the leaves may first be sewn upon green tape and afterwards tacked or glued upon the foundation; but when zinc forms the base the leaves may be fastened upon it with strong paste. When

Fig. 23.—Circles symbolising Eternity.

taken down the zinc should be dipped in water, when the leaves may be easily removed, leaving the zinc ready for another occasion.

Fig. 22 is the *Shield of Faith*, surrounded by a circle, the emblem of Eternity. When the shield is of zinc it may be painted in oil colours with a white ground and red cross. This also forms the cross of our patron saint, St. George. The circle may be covered with green leaves with a very happy result; a few red berries will add to the effect.

When the shield is of millboard, it may have white calico or paper pasted upon it, and the cross formed of either real or artificial red berries which can be glued upon it. Or the shield may be covered with strong paste and the cross first covered with red berries and the four quarters covered with white everlasting flowers or rice. The circle around the shield may first be coated with paste and then covered with dry, grey moss.

Fig. 23. *Circles* symbolising Eternity. The circles may be covered so as to be distinct, by arranging them thus : one of red berries or red immortelles, one of white ever-lastings and one of violet everlastings. Violet is the colour

Fig. 24.—Greek Cross on a
Double Triangle.

for Advent but not entirely inappropriate for Christmas. If preferred, box leaves may take the place of the latter.

Fig. 24. The *Greek Cross* upon double triangles makes a very effective device if the latter are covered in two tints of leaves, pale and dark green, and the cross formed of holly berries or red everlastings—or the arms of the cross may be formed of white everlastings, with red berries at the junction. Another plan is to cut the cross out of zinc and paint it red with the sacred monogram (I.H.S.) in the centre in white.

Fig. 25. The *Cross and Anchor,* typifying atonement and patience. This looks well entirely of green—dark leaves for the cross-anchor and golden leaves for the circle. Golden holly for the latter and variegated ivy for the former look well, but they must be made according to the material in hand. A little taste and judgment displayed upon the spot is frequently far preferable to ideas given in books, which are not in every case practicable, owing to lack of materials.

Fig. 26. *Cross and Scroll.* This device, by varying the text, may be made to do duty at any festival. It should be cut out of zinc and the scroll painted white so that coloured letters may be inscribed upon it. The cross may be covered

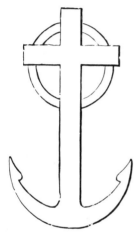

Fig. 25.—Cross and Anchor, symbolising Atonement and Patience.

Fig. 26.—Cross and Scroll with Text.

with paste and dry moss stuck upon it. Another plan is to paint the scroll a very pale green, form the letters of red berries, and cover the cross with cotton-wool carefully cut to shape with a pair of sharp scissors, after the adhesive has had time to dry.

Still another plan is to cover the scroll with red paper or calico, to form the letters of white immortelles or rice, and to cover the cross with small green leaves. The permutations of colouring and the materials appropriate for these devices are endless.

Fig. 27. A combination of *Trefoil* and *Triangle* (both
typical of the Trinity) and a unique *Maltese Cross* for centre
ornament, known to heralds as a *crosslet pattée.* It can be
made in many ways, and is effective in all. The outer part
may be made of millboard, upon which should be glued a
piece of calico or other material to form a background. If
the background is red the outer part of the device may be
green, and the device in the centre white immortelles, cotton
wool, rice, or frost. Whichever is selected may be glued or
pasted on a device cut from cardboard.

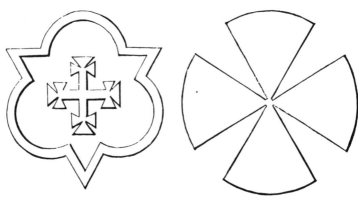

Fig. 27.—Combined Triangle and   Fig. 28.—Circular Maltese Cross.
Trefoil with Crosslet Pattée
in Centre.

Another way would be to cover the background with cotton-
wool, make the cross of red berries, and the outer frame of
moss glued on and neatly trimmed with scissors.

Fig. 28 is a *Maltese Cross* cut from a circle of zinc or millboard, and may be varied by making the end of each arm
concave instead of convex. It may be covered with dry
French moss, with white everlasting flowers or red immortelles, according to the background upon which it will be set.

Fig. 29. *Triangles and Cross in Circle.* This device
offers scope for varied treatment both as to colours and
materials used. We will give a mode of executing the device,

but a little thought will suggest a dozen different ways to the worker who is at all conversant with these matters. The cross (w) may be cotton wool; the background of red berries; the triangles (g) of any small evergreen leaves or of green everlastings, with red everlastings in the six little triangles forming a background (r). The large circle may be of white everlasting or Cape flowers, and the six pieces inside the circle (y) may be of straw tissue glued on and marked into rays with deep chocolate oil colour.

Fig. 30. *Foliated Cross* and *Monogram.* The centre design should be of straw tissue with the " I.H.S."* and

Fig. 29 —Device in Everlasting Flowers, Berries, &c., upon zinc or cardboard foundation.

Fig. 30.—Emblem to be worked in Moss, Everlasting Flowers, &c., on a wood, zinc, or cardboard base.

rays painted upon it in chocolate. The cross will look well in white everlasting flowers, the circle in red berries— perhaps a trifle narrower than shown in the illustration—and the four pieces forming the background of French moss.

Fig. 31. The *Star of Bethlehem.* This is a very simple but very effective device. Make the star of white everlastings or Cape flowers, the background of red immortelles and the circle of holly, box, or evergreen oak—the holly for preference. It should be placed in a conspicuous place in the chancel or on the front panel of the pulpit.

---

* The " C " is the ancient form of " S."

Fig. 32. This is a somewhat elaborate rendering of the *Monogram of the Creator*, A Ω, alpha and omega, the First and the Last. The foundation may be cut with a sharp stencil or mount-cutter's knife, and will require some amount of patience in the execution, as the millboard must be thick. When cut out melt some size, in it stir a little powdered whiting, and with this paint the device, going over it a second time when the first coat is dry.

When the second coat is dry the device A Ω may be painted on the inner circle with ordinary oil colours—chocolate letters on a golden background, or golden letters on a red background. The middle circle may in either case be white or a greenish-grey.

Fig. 31.—Star of Bethlehem, to be covered with Evergreens, Everlasting Flowers, &c.

Fig. 32.—Monogram of the Creator, to be painted, covered with Moss, &c.

Fig. 33.—Device cut from zinc or cardboard, to be picked out in Everlasting Flowers, &c.

The outer circle may be covered liberally and flatly with moss, carefully trimmed with sharp scissors, and the four crosses made of red immortelles. This is one mode, but it may be varied according to individual taste and the materials at hand.

For a companion device to this, our Saviour's *Monogram* I.H.S. may appear in the centre, and should a third be required the monogram in Fig. 33 may be used. It was the first monogram used by the early Christians, and was, as previously explained, displayed on the Labarum. It consists of the first two Greek letters in the name of Christ, xp, the x being placed on the downstroke of the p, as shown. Examples of this go back as far as the fourth century.

Fig. 33, *The Christian Monogram*, is a very simple form, It may be cut as a vesica-shaped device, with the letters marked in lead pencil as a guide, either from wood, millboard, or zinc, and may be worked thus : the letters should be of white and gold immortelles on a background of moss with the outer margin of red immortelles or very small everlastings. Or the letters may be red and green on a white wool background, and the outer border of yellow Cape flowers.

These devices may be used in many places in the church— as on the fronts of galleries, on the blank spaces between the windows, on the window-sills, on the pulpit or reading-desk, on the screen, and, indeed, anywhere where they show to advantage.

Scrolls and Texts.

SCROLLS, as distinct from *texts*—which are usually straight, whilst scrolls are curved and, being folded over, show their backs in places—are much used in church decoration, both permanently and temporarily, as in our case. They may either be illuminated by hand on zinc, or cut from stout cartoon paper if small, or from linoleum if large, and fastened in position after having been lettered.

If the scrolls are of either paper or zinc, the parts which turn over must be coloured so as to differentiate from the front. If of zinc, the front of the material must be coated with two coats of ordinary white paint—simply ready-mixed house paint, costing 4d. per lb. The letters may then be cut out of any materials chosen and glued on, and a border of evergreens added. If cartoon paper is chosen, the " turn-overs " must be coloured different from the front, and if of linoleum the front of the scroll must be painted, leaving the " turn-overs " of their natural brown colour.

TEXTS form a very considerable portion of the work at all festivals, as they are meant to voice the feelings of the worshippers, and to give emphasis to the decorations themselves : they speak, as it were, the wishes, praises, and thanks of the congregation. A straight text in architectural parlance is called a "label." The foundations or backgrounds for the lettering are various : (1) A light deal frame of wood, ¾in. by 3in., halved together at the corners and secured with short screws. This may be covered with (2) paper ; (3) calico, linen, or other textile ; (4) with velvet ; (5) or white swansdown. It may be made of (6) half-inch deal boards, painted any desired colour ; (7) of strips of oilcloth, linoleum, or kamptulicon, which must be first sized and then painted ; (8) of zinc cut to shape and afterwards painted.

Any of these backgrounds, from paper to velvet, may be selected according to the funds at disposal.

(2) Paper. This may be lining paper, continuous cartoon paper, certain kinds of wall paper, flock, or raised paper, or some of the figured paper with raised surface of a decorative character.

(3) Calico, &c. The textile backgrounds are very numerous, among them being calico, plain and glazed, linen, union, plain or coloured, twill, thin buckram, flannel, flannelette, rep, &c.

(4) Velvet, cotton velvet, Utrecht, and stamped velvet. These are all very expensive, and would only be suitable for using as pulpit panels, &c., for a background for the sacred monogram, or for banners.

(5) Swansdown makes a lovely background for letters of any colour or material, having a dull surface for pasting down and a beautiful flossy, white surface as a bed for the letters—but it is expensive.

(7) Kamptulicon is a very thick material, and only suited for very large texts. Neither of the three floor-coverings

recommended need be new, as old pieces when painted are indistinguishable from new.

The mode usually adopted to form the letters is to cut them out of paper, either white or coloured, and stick them upon the background.

To form the letters correctly it will be found helpful to cut out the alphabet—or those letters which will be required—from thin cardboard, to a standard size, say 4in. or 6in. high; and when a text is selected the pattern letter is laid on the material and a pencil run round it, leaving the shape of the letter. By this means one person can keep several others employed with scissors or sharp stencil knife cutting out the letters required.

Fig. 1 (page 8) will show how the letters are formed on a groundwork of one-inch squares. In this case the letters will be 6in. high, but if 4in. letters are required the squares must be made proportionately smaller.

In fastening the letters upon the background two things are absolutely necessary—that the letters are perfectly upright, and that they are properly spaced. A dot of the same colour as the letters placed between each word is effective but not absolutely necessary.

A good plan is to have two thin pieces of twine as chalk-lines, one rubbed with white chalk and the other with charcoal. The height of the letter having been marked at each end of the background, the string is held securely at each end, exactly over the marks, and then gently raised in the centre and " twanged " down, when a perfectly true straight line will be left, which may easily be removed, after the letters are fixed, by means of a duster.

Use a T-square in fixing the letters, so as to secure uprightness. If you do not possess a T-square, fold a piece of paper of any shape in two, then fold it again so that the folded edges are one above the other when pressed down, and you have a correct set-square. By the way, should you require a rule and do not happen to have one, you may easily make one with a half-penny, which is exactly an inch in diameter.

When the letters are in place the next thing is to add a border, and for this purpose adequate space should be left at top and bottom of the letters. The general rule is that the background should be twice the height of the letters. Thus if the background is 12in. high, the letters should be 6in., leaving a space of 3in. both at top and bottom.

Letters should, of course, be of a colour contrasting with the background, and may be formed of many materials. Evergreen leaves may be pasted on to form them; in which case the letters must be carefully outlined with a lead pencil before commencing. Everlasting or Cape flowers may be employed, and these, according to the colour of the background, may be used either in their natural colour of a glossy white or dyed.

Flock paper, ordinary white or coloured paper, or gold or silver paper may also be used; but in the latter case a broad chocolate or black outline to throw the letters into relief will be necessary. Ordinary artist's oil colour will do for this purpose if thinned with a little gold-size varnish and turpentine, both of which act as driers. White cotton-wool letters on a green or red ground look well. To prepare these, first cut out the letters in cardboard and coat them with adhesive. Next lay a sheet of cotton-wool on your work-table glazed side uppermost, and press the coated letter firmly upon it, afterwards roughly cutting the letter from the rest of the sheet and laying it aside to dry. When quite dry—a little artificial heat will hasten matters—cut off the superabundant wool, square and neatly, along the edge of the cardboard letter, and it is ready for the background.

Another plan, after the cardboard letters have been cut out and coated with paste, is to fasten dry moss upon them and trim off with sharp scissors, or they may be covered thickly with rice to form very pretty silvery white letters. If sufficient rice does not adhere at first, apply a second coat of gum and more rice, until a rough, rugged surface is formed. When thoroughly dry the capital letters may be covered with gold paint, when they will have a very pretty, " nubbly " effect, resembling virgin gold. Evergreens pasted on the cardboard have a capital appearance, and any outstanding edges of leaves may be removed without having any unsightly effect—still, great care should be exercised so that the leaves do not overhang the edge of the cardboard letters. Then there are " white frost " letters made by sprinkling " frost," which may be bought in packets, upon white cardboard letters, which have first been brushed over with weak gum. A saturated solution of Epsom salts brushed over anything to be " frosted " will, on drying, crystallise and give a very realistic appearance. (See also page 57.)

Straw tissue is both easy to cut and very effective in appearance, and is to be recommended for lettering. It is sold in sheets about 21in. by 8in., and costing about 9d. each, or 8s. per dozen sheets. It also forms a capital background for coloured or evergreen letters. Letters cut from it are simply pasted on and weighted down till dry. Helichrysums make chaste, pearly-looking letters, but when used the black seed should first be removed from the centre and the flower either held in steam or before a fire to open it. It should then be flattened out and applied to the work in hand.

Borders to surround the texts may be of evergreens sewn upon green tape, and then fastened in position round the lettering, with a few bright red berries dispersed here and there, or simply in the four corners. Borders of plaited coloured paper, if the colours are artistically chosen, have a pleasing appearance, but too many colours should not be used or a harlequin appearance will be the result. Everlasting Cape flowers—the large variety—make a fine border when alternated with evergreens, all of which may be pasted on. The Cape flowers look well when pasted on back upwards. A border of little diamonds, tre-foils, quatrefoils, cinque-foils, circles, and other devices cut from paper has a fair effect if the devices are kept the same size and put on level, but they are too flat to tell out well. Good taste will suggest many forms of border, the materials at disposal rendering the form in which they may be used almost endless.

ILLUMINATED TEXTS.—For a foundation for these there is a choice of several materials. A deal frame may have a piece of painted linen or calico stretched upon it, or the worker may make his own "canvas," which comes less expensive. For this purpose strain a piece of white buckram calico over the frame by tacks round the edge. Go over it with size melted in hot water, to which a little powdered whiting has been added, and when dry paint it with ordinary white house paint, thinned out with turpentine (use no more oil or a glossy surface will be produced). Allow that to dry, and give it a second coat, which, when dry, will be ready to work upon.

The resultant effect should be the production of a flat white surface with little or no gloss upon it. The white need not be absolutely cold and colourless, but may have a suspicion of cream tone in it, which may be produced by adding a pinch of chrome yellow to the colour. Commence by setting out the letters required to form a text; this may be best managed by drawing faint pencil lines of the height of the contemplated letters quite across the background and within that space either sketching out the letters, if facile with the pencil, or marking round cardboard letters, which will probably be quicker and more certain. The various letters are next to be painted in with a camel or sable hair brush and ordinary oil colour thinned with turpentine. If the colours are fairly deep in tone they will stand out well from a pale background, but if the colours of the letters and background approximate too closely the letters will appear indistinct when placed at a distance from the eye. To remedy this it will be necessary to trace a black or dark brown outline round each letter; the line should for a 4in. letter be an eighth of an inch thick and for a 6in. letter a little wider.

If any golden letters are required they may either be gilded with ordinary " transferred gold leaf " or painted with one of the numerous gold paints so much advertised. Another plan is to apply japanner's gold size to the letter, allow it to dry until " tacky " to the touch, and then to sprinkle bronze powder over it. In any case, a broad dark line of colour must surround each letter to give it sharpness and distinctness.

The ordinary worker is frequently at a loss to know what kind of lettering he had better adopt for texts, and to help him we give in the Introduction four examples, one being specially designed for illuminating.

In illuminating or writing a " label " (straight) or " scroll " (curved) inscription, the employment of too many colours makes the whole text look tawdry and gives it a harlequin-like appearance. The best effect is gained by having red, deep green, or chocolate letters for the body of the words with ornamental capitals or initial letters, in which gold, black, and colours should play their part with excellent result. Clearness of letter rather than size is to be aimed at to gain legibility.

If the amateur decorator cannot manage the real gold or bronze powder he may gum or paste gold paper on the letter or part of the letter to be gilded and then with red, black, or chocolate colour, paint a good outline round it. The effect is very passable.

So as to afford a choice of texts both as to wording and length of sentence we herewith give a list of those most suitable, arranged in order of length.

Texts for Christmas.

" Behold your God."
" Gloria in Excelsis."

" The Lamb of God."

" The Prince of Life."

" He came unto His own."

" God sent forth His Son."

" The Light of the World."

" Behold, thy King cometh."

" The Author of Salvation."

" Emmanuel. God with us."

" God manifest in the Flesh."

" Hosanna to the Son of David."

" Thou shalt call His name Jesus."

" King of Kings and Lord of Lords."

" The Desire of all Nations shall come."

" Thou art the King of Glory, O Christ."

" Now is come Salvation, and Strength."

" We love Him because He first loved us."

" The day-spring from on high hath visited us."

" Unto us a Child is born, unto us a Son is given."

" Who for our salvation came down from Heaven."

" The Word was made Flesh and dwelt among us."

" The people that walked in Darkness have seen a great Light."

" The Lord shall give unto Him the Throne of His Father David."

" The right hand of the Lord bringeth mighty things to pass."

" He shall be great, and shall be called the Son of the Highest."

" Unto you is born this day a Saviour, which is Christ the Lord."

" The Son of Righteousness shall arise with healing in His wings."

" Glory to God in the Highest, on earth Peace, Goodwill toward men."

" The Root and Offspring of David, and the Bright and Morning Star."

" He came not to do His own Will, but the Will of Him that sent Him."

" There shall come a Star out of Jacob and a Sceptre shall arise out of Israel."

" There shall come forth a Root out of Jesse. and a Branch shall grow out of his Roots."

" He shall be called Wonderful, Counsellor, the Mighty God, the Everlasting Father, the Prince of Peace."

In addition to the texts required for Christmastide, texts are sometimes used for the Church seasons clustering around it, and for these we subjoin a few appropriate sentences :

TEXTS FOR ADVENT.

" Watch and pray."

" The Lord is at hand."

" Behold, a King shall reign."

" Hosanna to the Son of David! "

" He cometh to judge the Earth."

" The Day of Christ is at hand."

" Prepare ye the way of the Lord."

" Behold, thy King cometh unto thee."

" The Son of man shall come in His glory."

" Be ye also ready. The Son of man cometh."

" The Night is far spent, the Day is at hand."

" Behold, He cometh with clouds ; and every eye shall see Him."

" He shall come again in His glorious majesty to judge both the quick and the dead."

TEXTS FOR THE FEAST OF THE CIRCUMCISION.

" His name was called Jesus."

" Circumcision is that of the Heart."

" Circumcision is the keeping of the Commandments."

TEXTS FOR EPIPHANY.

" A Light to lighten the Gentiles."

" Arise, shine ; for Thy Light is come."

" Rejoice, ye Gentiles, with His people."

" The Gentiles shall see Thy righteousness."

" The Lord shall be thine everlasting Light."

" He shall bring forth judgment to the Gentiles."

" The people that walked in darkness have seen a great Light."

" The Gentiles shall come unto Thee from the ends of the earth."

" They presented Him gifts : gold, frankincense, and myrrh."

" We have seen His Star in the east, and are come to worship Him."

Trellises, &c., for Large Spaces.

Where large spaces have to be covered, evergreen trellis work is usually adopted, and this may be of many forms.

Perhaps the simplest kind is made by covering deal laths with evergreens and crossing them diagonally, tying them where they cross with iron wire or fastening them with a single screw. A straight, broad wreath on rope will finish off the top and link the upper ends of the laths together. The laths should first be painted green, or, if holly berries are scarce, red, so that little pieces of the laths peeping out here and there will have the same effect as red berries when seen at a distance. A little knot of berries fixed at each junction of the trellis will set off the whole design.

If the worker requires something more elaborate, Fig. 34 may be attempted. It is made with fine large leaves of evergreen and holly berries, and is suitable for chancel walls, either flanking the Communion table or upon the side walls. The foundation is first built up of a lattice or trellis of deal laths.

Commence by covering the trellis with yew, box, evergreen oak, arbor vitæ, privet, or other small leaves, fixing the various evergreens with thin wire. This will provide work for several persons.

Next take a quantity of holly berries, and with a needle and thread make several yards of coral-like beadwork. This gives employment to another helper. Whilst one is doing the coral work another may cut out a number of quatrefoils from straw tissue, and yet another may cut out a few elegant

Fig. 34.—Trellis of Evergreen for covering Walls.

little crosses from dark paper. Next proceed to sew the string of berries round the quatre-foils and to place them also upon the little crosses.

It only remains to fix these designs at the intersections of the trellis, and to fix the trellis against the wall, and the whole is complete. Such a device entails much time and patience, but where helpers are numerous the benefit so derived carries out the old adage : " Many hands make light work." The leader of the workers must, however, be on the alert to see that the general effect is uniform and harmonious.

Imitation Berries.

In almost all devices holly and ivy berries play a most important part, but it sometimes happens that berries are not very plentiful, and recourse has to be had to imitation ones. Fortunately the making of these is not a very difficult task, as we will show.

For the trellis work mentioned above some hundreds of holly berries would be required, and if natural berries are not readily obtainable, we can make them thus :

Procure 2oz. of best red sealing wax and powder it in a mortar, or strong earthen pot ; place it in a bottle, into which pour a quarter of a pint of strong spirits of wine : this will dissolve the wax and make a kind of red varnish. Shake the bottle well, but no heat need be applied. Have ready a pair of small forceps and a bag of peas, and dip the latter into a shallow saucer of the red varnish, taking care to keep it continually stirred ; dip several times, and the peas will gradually assume a more rubicund appearance until finally they are changed into very realistic holly berries.

A quicker plan is to place a handful of peas into a shallow saucer, pour a very little of the red varnish over them, and keep them rolling about until they are completely covered. Then rake them out upon a piece of paper and do the same with some more peas until enough have been coated. They must then be dried and coated again and again until they are of the desired redness. When finished they may be glued on the device.

Another way is to use red enamel paint instead of sealing wax varnish.

For ivy berries use peas, black sealing wax dissolved as before, or black enamel paint.

If the holly berries are to be used with stalks, cut off a great number of lengths of fine iron wire, each about 3in. long, and double them in the centre like a hairpin, but closer together. Take a piece of cotton wool, insert in the looped end and give it a turn or two so as to make a little knob as large as a holly berry. As one person does this they should be passed to a second to dip into hot size in which a little vermilion has been stirred. When dry, dip several times either in red sealing wax varnish or vermilion enamel paint, and allow them to dry. To finish put a little black paint on a piece of paper and taking the red berries up in bunches touch the apex on the paper, which will tip each with a little black dot, and so complete the artificial berries.

Ivy berries are made in the same way, the bloom being imitated by dusting the berries with a little blue or purple toned powder colour. For some devices rice may be made a substitute for berries by dyeing it scarlet with Judson's Dye.

Frost Work.

There are several ways of giving the effect of frost or rime upon twigs, leaves, and other objects, and as the effect produced is extremely good it may be utilized for devices in conspicuous places, such as the pulpit and reading desk.

The following is one of the most useful for twigs and branches. Round the leafless twigs roll some untwisted lamp cotton, making them as rough and rustic as possible. Next make a mixture of 1lb. of alum to a quart of water, and boil until the alum is perfectly dissolved. When done, pour into a deep pan. In this liquid suspend by wires the branches to be frosted or crystallised, being careful that they do not touch the sides of the pan and that every twig is immersed. Leave them so suspended for twenty-four hours, when they will be coated with a capital imitation of frost.

Another plan is to lay the sticks down and give the upper surface a touch of white oil colour paint, which must be thoroughly dry before the various pieces are suspended in the mixture.

Epsom salts dissolved in water in the same way as alum also makes good " frost." The solution must be very strong to give good results. Crystallised Epsom salts can be used in another way. Melt some gum tragacanth or isinglass and coat the objects to be frosted; whilst still wet

Fig. 35.—Anchor of Hope, in Moss and Everlasting Flowers.

Fig. 36.—Latin Cross, in Cape and other Everlasting Flowers.

dust the salts thickly over with a small sieve, and the result will be a sparkling one.

There are several kinds of " frost " sold, and among them one which is peculiarly brilliant. It is known as " Frosted Glass Shavings "—but it is really crushed white glass, which should be fastened to the objects with strong white glue. Cover the surface to be frosted with the glue and powder the " frost " upon it by means of a small wire sieve, shaking off the residue and saving it for a future occasion.

Everlasting Flower Devices.

The dried flowers used for this purpose are dealt with on pages 26 and 27.

What are known as Fairy flowers—a very large kind of everlasting—form terminals for crosses or centres for many devices and are very beautiful. When without wires " everlastings " may be fastened to the foundation of the devices with strong paste or glue.

Fig. 35 shows a device in moss and everlasting flowers, the *Anchor of Hope*. It is formed upon a zinc, wood, or millboard base, and is intended for a device not more than

Fig. 37.—A Holly Crown.

Fig. 38.—A Crown of Victory.

30in. high. Tiny leaves jutting from the moss will set off the background to greater advantage.

Fig. 36 makes a handsome *Latin Cross* as follows: Cut the cross out of two pieces of deal, halved and screwed in the centre. Cover with red velvet or plush and upon it glue a row of white immortelles all round, finishing with Cape and Fairy flowers as shown.

Fig. 37, a *Holly Crown*. Make this upon a piece of wood shaped like a shuttle, upon which is affixed a piece of red twill having the top part unfastened. In this pocket arrange the holly, natural leaves, and berries, and glue down. The letters may be on white cardboard with a row of large white everlastings at top and bottom. The inner surface—shown at bottom—may be covered with moss or box leaves.

Fig. 38, a *Crown of Victory*.   On a wooden or zinc foundation glue a piece of deep crimson material, flock paper, or cotton velvet, and glue fine, smooth holly leaves upon it as shown.   Next put on the little circles either with holly berries or immortelles.   The base is first to be covered with bay or box leaves, and finished with fine white or coloured Cape flowers, glued on back upward, in which position they have the best effect.   These are intended for jewels.

Fig. 39.—The Star of Bethlehem—suitable for the Pulpit.

Fig. 39, the *Star of Bethlehem*.   This forms a very appropriate design for the centre panel of the pulpit or other important position.   Millboard, zinc, or wood may be used for the foundation, which should afterwards be covered with straw tissue, the flutes running outward towards the points as shown.   First glue on a border of small red everlastings as in the design, adding a Fairy or Cape flower at the tip of each ray and a very large one at the junction of the rays.   Next with some fine large laurel leaves of dark green form the star or circle in the centre, and upon it place another circular device of golden holly leaves, finishing the centre with a circle of artificial holly berries on wires, the

bundle of wires being thrust through a hole in the foundation and fastened at the back. With any desired variation
of colouring this makes a handsome device, very appropriate to the season.

Banners.

Banners meant as devices are somewhat different from
those used for processional purposes; they need not be of

Fig. 40.—Simple Banner for decorating
Columns, Wall Spaces, &c.

such costly material; they need no poles, and they may have
linoleum, millboard, or deal frames for the foundations.

Fig. 40 is a very simple device for placing on the pillars
of the nave or upon the spaces between the windows. Its
foundation may be a sheet of millboard cut to shape and
covered with prepared cloth, or the millboard may be first
sized and then painted with ordinary white paint, if the
ground it hangs against is dark, or of any appropriate colour

if the wall or pillar is white. In the latter case the surface
may be covered with coloured paper.

The device of the cross and circular label may then be
painted upon it, and evergreen leaves, set in fours, may be
pasted on, as shown in the upper corners. Or the leaf
work may continue all round the banner. A border of pairs
of leaves set herring-bone fashion also has a capital effect.

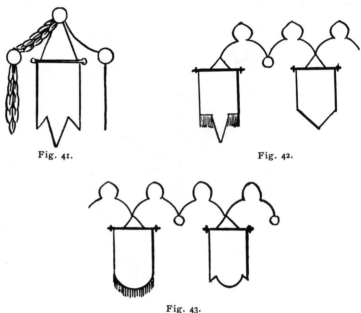

Fig. 41.   Fig. 42.

Fig. 43.

Suggestions for Cutting out and Arranging Banners.

Banners should be about two-thirds as wide as they are
high. They look best when fairly tall for the width rather
than short, as in the latter case they have a squat, dumpy,
inartistic appearance. The form of the banner and its
arrangement should vary, to give relief to the monotony of
the same shape being in evidence all round the church. Figs.
41 to 43 show variations, but a little thought given to the
subject will evolve many other shapes.

Fig. 44, *Bethlehem*, is a banner out of the ordinary stereotyped pattern, and may be painted in oils on a piece of oilcloth, linoleum, or kamptulicon. Whichever of these is chosen should first be cut to shape, sized, and painted with two coats of white paint, when it is ready for the illuminator's hands.

The quaint buildings of the city, wall, &c., may be coloured grey with some red in the roofs; the foreground warm ochre and brown, with green grass; the sky a very pale Cambridge blue, and the peculiar clouding a warm purple-grey. The star and rays should be gilded, or, if real gold cannot be manipulated, gold paper cut to shape and pasted on must be used. Deep chocolate should be used as the colour for the border lines, and the outer margin may be red.

A round stick with ornamental knobs at the ends should be wired to the back for sus- pending the banner, and it may be finished at the bottom with coloured worsted fringe. Such

Fig. 44.—Banner for Christmas, painted in oils.

a banner should be carefully packed away wrapped in paper when the decorations are taken down for the season, as being on lasting material and painted in oil colour it should last for many years.

Besides stiff material, banners may be painted on " pre- pared cloth," either calico or linen, or upon American cloth, which is procurable in various colours, also in gold and silver, and any desired devices may be painted thereon in oil colours.

Fig. 45, *Banner of the Magi*, shows the three vases representing the gifts of gold, frankincense, and myrrh, beneath the rays of the Star of Bethlehem. This is a device that might be appropriately painted on American gold cloth, the background being in chocolate or dark green, leaving the charges in relief. These will then only require a little shading to complete them. On the little label behind the lower vase space may be found for the words, " The Magi " or " The Wise Men."

However beautiful the design may be, a banner on a bare

Fig. 45.—Banner of the Magi and Garland of Evergreens
for placing on space between windows.

wall has a naked, forlorn appearance. To obviate this and to frame the picture or device, it will be found advisable to place round it a garland of evergreens as shown in the illustration.

For this purpose fairly large leaves of laurel may be employed, with perhaps a bunch of berries upon the centre, from which the banner depends, whilst the garland itself may be tied and suspended by a large bow of coloured ribbons contrasting and brightening the deep hue of the evergreens.

Fig. 46, *Stars and Palms.* This emblem should be used only about the chancel, either upon a banner or on an ordinary emblem, the palm being typical of victory, and the stars, in form of a crown, the Scriptural emblem of the Church. It may be enclosed in an evergreen circle, the emblems being placed on a background of red flannel, velvet, flock paper, or other material. The palm branches may be the real article or dried leaves fastened to suitable branches and interspersed with white berries. The stars may be of cardboard encrusted with "glass frost," mica scales, or other frosting medium.

Fig. 46.—Device showing Crown of Stars and Palm Branches.

The Lectern.

Another suitable place for the " stars and palms " (Fig. 46) is on the eagle lectern or reading-desk, on which the conquering Bible rests. The support of the lectern should be decorated with handsome garlands of variegated holly, twisted spirally around it, and the base hidden with Christmas roses in pots, or cut flowers placed in little extinguisher-shaped zinc flower holders filled with water. These can rise from and be hidden by a bed of moss, fir, and other evergreens.

The Pulpit.

This varies considerably in form in different churches, and it is impossible to give descriptions that will be

F

applicable to all, but it is hoped that the following hints will be found useful in most cases, or that something at least may be learned from them.

A bold wreath of holly, set with many berries in bunches, may encircle the top of the pulpit. Let tape be used as a foundation and the berries be put on after the wreath is

Fig. 47.—Design for Pulpit Decoration, principally in
Evergreens and Everlasting Flowers.

hung in place, as they can then be fixed just where they are most telling.

The panels may be filled with moss pasted on cardboard which has been made to fit them. If there should be no panels, still cardboard plaques may be covered with moss or rich green flock paper, and the different devices fastened on, the edges being concealed with a small wreath of box leaves, or a border of twisted straw plait will answer the same purpose admirably.

In Fig. 47 an example is given of pulpit decoration. For devices in the panels a choice may be made from the following : The monogram I.H.S., double triangles, A Ω, vases containing the offerings of the Magi, the Lamb, short texts on scrolls, the anchor, the Star of Bethlehem (with five points), palm branches, the Crown of Victory, the Harp of Praise, crossed trumpets (heralding the birth of our Lord), a cradle with star over it, the Maltese or other cross, or any other appropriate device. (See also p. 119.)

For scrolls, only space for very short texts can be obtained, but the following may be suggested, " Prince of Peace," " Lamb of God," " Son of David," " Star of Jacob," " Peace on Earth," " Goodwill towards Men," " Child and King."

Beneath the panels another wreath should be placed, this time of firs, hot-house ferns, if available, and dyed grasses. Ferns or bracken, if gathered in the autumn, may be pressed and preserved for Christmas, and if not of good colour may be dipped in a vivid shade of Judson's green dye to correct the faded tone.

Pillars and balustrading may be twined with wreaths and tendrils of ivy, and the lower parts surrounded with feathery dried palms placed thickly against a background of green or red calico, or dried and dyed ferns may be used, or a pile of fir branches covered with imitation snow looks well— the snow being represented by brushing the upper parts with gum and dipping them in flour or powdered whiting.

A robin and a crossbill are sometimes shown in continental churches perched upon the snow-covered fir branches with very good effect, giving a pointed allusion to the pretty legends attached to those birds. Whether the introduction of birds into decorations would be thought good taste in England we cannot say; it is mentioned as a suggestion merely.

Gas or Lamp Standards.

These may be simply decorated with various kinds of evergreens made up into wreaths, and fastened with coloured ribbons to give brilliancy and relief to the dark leaves. To avoid monotony different leaves should be employed on the different standards. Any kind of evergreen is permissible for decorations.

The Chancel Screen.

Upon this a wealth of neat evergreen garlands may be shown interspersed with sacred devices (Figs. 21 to 33) in the various compartments. Banners may grace the doorway of the screen, but should not be displayed in the chancel itself ; the banner, suggesting a military trophy, finds no place in the abode of peace. For further information the reader is referred to the instructions given under " Harvest," page 138.

The Chancel Arch.

This gives ample space for a fine scroll with a text upon it, either of evergreen letters or illuminated ones, and for the purpose a long text may be chosen which can be read from any part of the church. If the foundation of the scroll is made of stout cartoon paper it will only last for one display, but if it is made of linoleum or zinc it will last for years, and may be freshly illuminated or lettered with straw tissue, red calico, or evergreens as required—so that the same text does not appear always in the same place.

The Stalls.

These, especially the ends facing the nave, must have much attention. Circular garlands with a shield in the centre may be hung at the ends. Wreaths in festoons, interspersed with flowers (if available) may garnish the fronts, and a double row of greenhouse plants ranged on either side

will look well. For further information the reader is referred
to " Easter " (page 88) and " Harvest " (page 141).

The Communion Table.

Very little decoration for this particular part of the church
is usually attempted, a beautiful white cross being all that
is really needful. This may be made of white azaleas and
ferns, but if, as sometimes happens, real flowers cannot be
procured, recourse must be had to artificial ones.

A very pretty cross is that shown in Fig. 48 ; it is composed wholly of Fairy flowers and dried
grasses. The Fairy flower is a very
beautiful one resembling a ball of floss
silk, and when placed on a background
of dried ferns, grasses, &c., has a very
handsome appearance. If the dried
leaves and grasses are not at hand use
real evergreens. A suitable text along
the front of the covered table will not
be at all out of place.

Decorate the sill of the East and
other windows, Communion rails, walls,
choir stalls, and other surroundings as
much as you please, but let the decoration of the actual table be very simple.

Fig. 48.—Cross of dried
Grasses and Fairy
Flowers for the Com-
munion Table.

The Font.

It is usual to leave the font decorations until the last ;
indeed the final arrangements, so far as real flowers are
concerned, are best left until Christmas morning, so as to
have them absolutely fresh. Very great taste may be displayed. Here is one scheme of decoration that has been
tried with every satisfaction.

Provide a tray to fit into the basin, level with the rim, and
on it place a snow cross, about 18in. high, rising from the
centre. Make the cross of wood about 2in. square,

cover it thickly with cotton wool, and with judgment pull out the wool to give it the uneven appearance and the lightness of snow. Allow some of the wool to hang from the arms of the cross like icicles.

With a soft brush touch the upper part with gum, on this dredge one of the various kinds of " frost," and leave it to dry. When dry, fix the cross in the centre of the tray, and round it wreath a string of fine red holly berries. The cross may stand on three steps, round which natural flowers springing from moss should be placed, but with their stems in zinc water tubes of the smaller kind, about 3in. high and costing 2s. 6d. per dozen.

The flowers used must all be white, such as Christmas roses, cyclamens, camellias, hyacinths, deutzias, &c.

The panels of the font if plain may be filled with moss on millboards, each with a little sacred device in the centre of white and red.

Round the stem, on the top step, a few pots of ferns may be placed, and the step itself covered with dark French moss, with stars of scarlet flowers laid upon it. This plan of somewhat heavy colouring serves as a foil to the pale colours employed upon the upper portion of the font, and a happy result is thus secured.

Sometimes the font is filled with water and a white cross made to float on the surface by being placed in a zinc trough, other star-shaped troughs containing white or pink flowers being floated around it and kept in their proper places by means of wires.

A pretty device is to form a hoop of hazel or ash saplings, just large enough to lie on top of the font, and from it arch other thin saplings so as to form a kind of dome or crown; this should then be wreathed in pale coloured evergreens having zinc flower holders attached, in which, on Christmas morning, cut white flowers may be placed and the whole finished on top with a bouquet of Christmas roses and real fern fronds.

Christmas. 71

Gallery Fronts.

These should have a wreath of evergreens depending in festoons from the top rail, and a straight wreath along the base. Angels playing musical instruments are very appropriate subjects for the panels.

The Frontispiece shows one of a set of Angels ringing bells. Such designs would form an excellent series, and would be best painted upon panels of linoleum, as if they were well executed, they would be worth preserving for future occasions. Let the Angels be clothed in white, with crimson wings (varied in colour), and the bells be of gold, with chocolate lettering, " Peace," " Praise," " Joy," "All

Fig. 49.—Shields hung on Festoon of Evergreens.

hail," " Jesu," " Alleluia," etc. The background should be pale blue.

Window Sills.

These should be bordered with evergreens and sacred emblems worked in everlasting flowers, moss, and evergreens for laying in the centre of each sill. Any of the devices mentioned in this section will serve for the purpose, notably Figs. 21 to 33. For further information the reader is referred to page 86.

Illuminated Shields and Devices.

Shields are useful for many purposes; they may be hung on pillars or gas standards, form the centres of evergreen devices, hang from long festooned wreaths (as in Fig. 49); or, if painted on a large scale, may be garlanded round, and the garlands set off with ribbons and everlasting flowers (as shown in Fig. 45, page 64).

Shields and kindred devices are best painted on zinc, and are usually cut in the old " flatiron " shape as shown. To prepare the zinc it is necessary to give it a couple of coats of ordinary white house paint, smoothing each coat with a piece of No. oo sandpaper or a piece of used emery-cloth. First sketch out the design to be illuminated on a piece of thin paper, and having obtained a fair outline, place the pattern upon a piece of soft wood or folded blotting-paper, and prick it all round with a pin; then put it on the

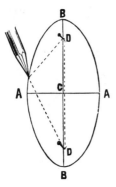

Fig. 50.—Method of drawing an Oval.

zinc shield and pounce through. Two pounces will be necessary, and they may be made thus : Place powdered whiting in a piece of old stocking or other loose material, and tie it up as one would a small pudding; in the other place lamp-black or finely-powdered charcoal. Where the shield is white dab the paper over with the black pounce, and where the ground is coloured use the white one. Where several devices of the same pattern have to be painted, this method saves much time. Correct the outline or add detail with a lead pencil, and paint in the devices with artists' oil-colours.

A crimson monogram on a white ground tells out well, and to frame it up a border of box or other leaves may be pasted on all round. Crimson backgrounds, with white and gold devices, are also effective; but in colouring, individual taste will suggest much. When the painting of the shields has thoroughly dried, each shield should be bent to a convex form, but not too much. They should never be varnished, or the glint of lights from different angles will destroy the effect.

In making devices it is sometimes necessary to form an

oval, and as this particular shape seems to be difficult to many, we may point out an easy mode of accomplishing the task. Glance at Fig. 50, and proceed as follows :

Draw a horizontal line A A the width of the desired oval, and a vertical line B B of the height the oval is to be made. Where the lines meet at C is the centre; from it take the distance C B with a pair of compasses, and placing one leg at A, carry it round until it cuts the vertical line at D at top, and D at bottom. Into these two points D D stick a couple of pins, and over them pass a circle of twine which from the lower D will reach to the top of the oval at B. Place the point of a pencil in the loop, and draw a line that will be formed by the string being pressed out to its full extent. A perfect oval will be the result. The dotted line represents the twine.

Remember that it is better to decorate too little than too much ; that all decorations should be made appropriate and suitable to the size of the church and its furnishing ; and, lastly, that the work should be done reverently, and not be looked upon as a pastime or a mere social function.

In concluding the portion treating upon Christmas decoration we may say that much of it will be applicable to other festivals—that it to say, the mode of using the various materials and the manner of making texts, wreaths, and other devices. It therefore behoves those who wish to decorate for other festivals to read first what has been written in the Christmas section.

Easter.

DECORATING the church at Easter, which a generation ago was but feebly carried out, has now become a recognised and general institution, and at no season of the year is it more appropriate. The joy of our hearts at the Resurrection of our Saviour—the seal of the completion of His work on earth—must surely be even greater than on the festival of His birth. The festival, coming as it does in early spring, is best commemorated by the use of as many flowers as possible; they have endured the darkness of earth and the severity of winter, and now break forth in a manner that is typical of the Resurrection.

Easter, of course, gives more scope for church decoration than the mid-winter festival of Christmas; and looking upon it as the outward sign of the return of our Lord to His Church on earth, we should use as many emblematic devices as possible, and everything that is suggestive of the renewal of life and of victory over death. The holly, as an emblem of winter, must not be employed, the darker-leaved evergreens generally should be avoided as much as possible, heavy wreaths should be discarded, and the wreaths or garlands used should be thinner and paler.

Wreaths.

As at Christmas wreaths form the backbone of the decorations, so do they at Easter; but they must now be made daintier and narrower. Golden laurel leaves may be made into an effective wreath by picking them from their stems and sewing them on green tapes or cut lengths of calico. They should be laid on as they grow—one leaf opposite another—but should be so arranged that they slightly lap at the sides and that the tip of the lower leaf covers the stalk of the one above it. The advantage of this kind of wreath is that it is very light and airy in effect, and can be affixed to a wall with

Fig. 51.—Trellis pattern in Evergreens, &c., for Chancel Arch or for surrounding Windows.

any slender nails. It looks well around windows, as a trellis, for entwining columns, etc.

A few thin hooks driven into the interstices between the joints of bricks or masonry, on gallery fronts and other places, may be left permanently in position, as they will not be seen unless looked for especially. The wreaths and devices may then be tied to the hooks with coloured tape, twine, or wire, and so an endless driving of nails year after year may be

avoided.   One or two nails or hooks placed at the top and
bottom of a pillar will generally be found sufficient to retain
the wreaths, and can be so placed as not to require removing.

The Chancel Arch.

Fig. 51 shows an idea for embellishing the chancel arch
or windows.   It should be made entirely of one sort of

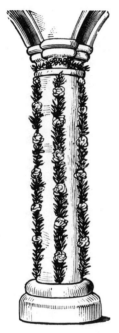

Fig. 52. — Method of Decorating
Pillars   with   perpendicular
Wreaths   of   Evergreens   and
Flowers.

Fig. 53. — A neat Wreath
suitable for Small Pillars
or for Pulpit-front.

leaf, and have bunches of daffodils, primroses, or yellow
everlastings at every crossing.   It may be made upon rather
stout wire or thin wood shaped to the curve of the arch.   If
used for a series of windows along the nave, they should be
connected by the same design being continued along the wall
above the dado, from window to window.

The Pillars.

In making wreaths in springtime, the newly-formed leaves
of trees and shrubs should not be used, as they die almost
immediately, being immature.   Golden laurel, being one of the
brightest of evergreens, is recommended for Easter wreaths,
especially the smaller and paler kinds.   Laurel wreaths, set
with either real or artificial flowers, may be placed upon the
columns as in Fig. 52, where they are treated in straight lines
between the base and capital.   They should be made on light
deal laths cut a trifle longer than the height of the column, so
that they may be " sprung" into place. A single piece of thin
twine or wire midway up the column will hold them all in
place.   Unless the column is one of the massive Norman ones,
four wreaths will be sufficient, but large columns will require
more.

Fig. 53 shows a neat wreath for pillars or pulpit front, for
placing round windows, &c.   It is formed with evergreen
leaves—golden laurel for choice—coloured calico, tape, and
everlasting flowers.   A long strip of coloured calico or
flannelette is first cut, either with straight sides or scalloped,
and upon it leaves of any suitable pale evergreen are sewn in
pairs as shown, and to hide the stalk-ends a piece of green
tape an inch wide is folded lightly down the centre and tacked
on to give the appearance of an outstanding stem.   Between
each pair of leaves flowers should be placed (small Cape
everlastings glued on a circle of coloured cloth will do as
well as any), and the wreath is complete.   For variety, the
colours of the various materials may be changed.   Such a
wreath has a very neat appearance—possibly too precise, but
certainly very effective.

Two lines of this device, having different colours, may be
placed round the chancel arch, if it is not too large, or
round the East or side windows of the nave.

Figs. 54 and 55 show other ways of garnishing pillars or
columns, the first being by spiral wreaths worked on a wire
or tape foundation, and the second by a combination of

horizontal and diagonal wreaths.   If the column diminishes
in bulk from bottom to top, the fastening at base and capital
will be almost sufficient to support them in place.   If not, a
band of thin white wire here and there round the column
will make everything secure.

To break the monotony of the evergreen, a little bunch of
white immortelles (gnaphaliums) may be introduced here and
there, or little ties, knots, or bows of pale ribbon, with droop-
ing ends, look very well, or white flowers may be used.   For
Ascension Day daisies in bunches are suitable.   As these

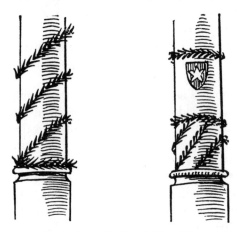

Figs. 54 and 55.—Suggestions for Garnishing Pillars with Wreaths.

would be fixed in bunches on the wreaths, after they
are finished it will be very little trouble to remove faded
flowers and replace with fresh ones.   Nothing is in worse
taste than dead flowers, and if workers find it too much
trouble to renew them, natural flowers should not be allowed
to form part of the scheme of decorations in the first place.
If the flower-stalks are surrounded by wet moss before being
thrust into the wreath they will keep fresh for a long time.

Ground ivy fastened on thin wire and entwined around
the pillars will be found light and appropriate for the

season, and pillars thus decorated can be finished at
the base, if this shows, by laying fresh moss around
them to a height of about six inches, and placing in
it, as if they were growing, natural flowers; those of the
small yellow celandine look very well. These little flowers
are usually abundant at Easter time, with the prim-
rose, violet, and others. The celandine flowers may be
gathered a month before Easter and pressed between blotting
paper, when they will be found to last much longer than
freshly-plucked flowers. A sunny day must be selected to
gather them, as they are then fully open, whereas in dull
weather they are partially closed. If tubes of water can be
inserted under the moss so much the better, as the pretty
little star-like yellow flower will then keep for a considerable
time.

Texts.

For texts, the best plan is to have a frame of deal made
to the size required, and to cover this with some kind of
suitable material. Of course the colour of the background
must be in contrast with the colour of the letter to be placed
upon it, and a choice may be made of cartoon paper, twill,
rep, white or coloured calico, serge, alpaca, white glazed
buckram, calico, or flannel. Flannelette is almost too poor.
Whichever material is chosen, it should be stretched over and
fastened to the frame with tinned tacks. Lines showing the
height of the letter to be fixed upon it should then be ruled
across the surface, with a piece of finely pointed chalk if the
material is coloured, or with a fine pencil if it is white.

The letters may be cut from cartridge-paper, white linen,
white calico, straw tissue, or other pale material for mount-
ing on a coloured ground, or from coloured wall-paper (flock
or plain), or almost any coloured fabric for a white ground.
They may be formed of pale evergreens, everlasting flowers,
gold paper, cotton-wool, or other material that may suggest
itself. Suitable letterings are shown on pages 8 to 14.

BORDERS may be formed of two different coloured materials twisted together and tacked on with small tinned tacks ; or of evergreen leaves, first sewn on tape, and then tacked on the frames in the same way. To avoid too much sameness in evergreen borders they may be brightened up with little knots or bunches of daffodils, forget-me-nots, snowdrops, primroses, or other flowers ; but these, being perishable, should be twisted on wires, and fixed in place at the last moment.

When illuminated borders are used for texts for this festival, they should be of white, gold, blue, and red, those being the symbolic colours, and therefore appropriate to the season. White represents Righteousness and Purity ; gold, Glory ; blue, Peace, Heavenly Hope, Remembrance, and Adoption ; and red, Divine Love, Redemption, and Forgiveness.

Upon a white ground of cartoon paper or unglazed calico, the simplest border is a line or two, or even three lines, drawn in different widths and of different harmonising colours, with a neat device at each corner, or at stated intervals, to break the monotony.

Another plan is to paint a dark flat border all round the text, say 2in. wide, or more if the frame is above 1ft. wide, and upon it to paint in colour or gold a zig-zag line, or a series of diamonds or other devices, so close that the edges touch. Or upon the dark colour a line of everlasting flowers may be fixed, which gives a very good effect. Instead of painting the coloured border a strip of coloured calico or other material may be used, the lower edge being cut in scallops. A bordering of dried ferns and grasses has a very artistic effect, especially if glued on a broad red band. Such a border gives great scope for the display of taste.

Moss may be glued on a long band of calico, and that afterwards glued round the text, in which case fresh moss is far more effective than the dried French moss. Moss at this time of year is in its full beauty, and presents many varieties from which a selection may be made. The moss which resembles tiny fern leaves is better for devices, pulpit or chancel decoration, than the commoner straggling moss, which may be utilised for borders, &c., as it grows much higher and so looks more raised.

The letters for the text should be half the height of the background; thus, a 12in. background takes a 6in. letter, and as each letter occupies the same space in width (with one or two exceptions), the length of text suitable for the length of background may be pretty accurately gauged by measurements, or the letters themselves may be roughly cut from newspaper, and laid in position as a more exact test.

If the principal letters of the alphabet are first cut from cardboard they may be used as patterns from which to cut letters in any material by simply pencilling round the shape.

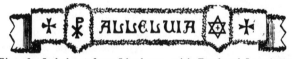

Fig. 56.—Label cut from Linoleum, with Bordered Inscription and Emblems.

Initial letters may be of different colour from the body of the text. For instance : on a white ground they may be of gold American cloth, with red calico or flock paper for the rest of the words. On another scroll there may be red initials and pale blue body letters ; and so on.

Kamptulicon or linoleum makes a capital background for texts, as it can be bought in any length, is easily cut, does not require a wooden frame to keep it flat, is impervious to damp, and will last, with ordinary care, for some years. The thinnest kind is best for the purpose, as it can be rolled up and put away ; besides which it is the cheapest, costing only 1s. 6d. to 2s. per square yard. It is also admirably adapted for banners, shields, and other devices, and should be more used than it is.

Fig 56 shows a way in which a piece of linoleum may be utilised to form a ground for a short text and several devices.

G

The letters may be of one colour and the emblems of another. The border should be of pale evergreens.

Fig. 57 is applicable to the curve of a window arch or the entrance to the chancel, and of course requires another one bending in an opposite curve to meet it, and so form a Gothic arch. The foundations of these and of Fig. 58 may be either of zinc or linoleum, and the letters may either be illuminated or formed of the leaves of the arbor vitæ, or box.

Fig. 57.—Curved Text for Window-arch or Chancel-arch.

Texts are sometimes placed around the walls of the nave or chancel without the use of any background, but this can only be done when the walls are of a colour to throw out the letters. Letters suspended with wires look better when made of leaves than when of almost any other material, as most other kinds of letters look poor and insignificant. Another plan is to stretch a long piece of red flannel or twill along the wall, and then, by sewing ivy or laurel leaves upon it, to form the text. Small ground ivy may be used for the letters and the variegated ivy or laurel for a bordering if desired. If this plan is adopted everything should be on a large scale. For a medium-sized church the background of red material should be quite 2ft. high and the letters 1ft., but if the nave is of large dimensions it may be a yard high and the evergreen letters eighteen inches.

Another plan is to use blue, red, or green calico, and to cut the letters from thin cardboard; or stout brown paper upon which white cotton wool is pasted and trimmed; while these in turn are pasted upon the background. The blue or green backgrounds are only suitable for a church with plenty of light, as so large a length of dark colour absorbs the light and renders the church and its decorations gloomy. Red backgrounds should be used for dark churches, unless the walls are of red brick, when a white or gold background will be best.

Straw tissue looks well for large letters on a coloured ground, being just enough tinted with gold to give a warm look, which is so conspicuously absent in white letters. For small texts for pulpits, reading desks, &c., straw tissue or straw-plait letters on a red cotton velvet ground have a rich, handsome appearance, but the expense is too great for large texts. For a border upon velvet, use straw tissue cut in curves or zig-zags, white or golden everlastings, or a narrow edging of arbor vitæ or box.

Small texts may be placed upon a back-ground of scrim-cloth, or coarse canvas, such as is used for packing. Of course it must be strained upon a deal frame before it can

Fig. 58.—Text for Window-arch or Chancel-arch.

be used. The material should be dipped in water and strained on the stretcher whilst wet; it will then dry as tight as a drum. Upon this coarse background moss or cotton-wool may be pasted, and upon whichever is chosen the letters, made of real flowers, may be placed. Letters made of silver Cape leaves upon a red flannel or moss background also look well.

Gold or silver paper pasted on cardboard is suitable for lettering if every letter has a good bold chocolate line painted round it.

Rice letters look well on a white wool ground if the rice is first died pink with a little cochineal or Judson's dye.

Paper rosettes form capital lettering, as the devices stand forth well and make bold and legible letters. Those of a cream colour should be chosen, as they give a beautiful ivory tone to the letters.

The materials and colours suitable for both backgrounds and letters are so numerous that a little ingenuity will provide many variations of the ideas and suggestions here embodied.

The texts suitable for the season of Lent and the festival of Easter are not so numerous as those appertaining to Christmas, but doubtless those we here give for Easter and the seasons around may be substantially extended.

Texts for Lent.

" God be merciful unto us.''

" Have mercy upon us, O Lord.''

" Spare Thy people, good Lord.''

" Let the wicked forsake his way.''

" His mercy is on them that fear Him.''

" Thou God of Hosts, look down from Heaven.''

" The sacrifices of God are a broken spirit and a contrite heart.''

Texts for Good Friday.

" It is finished.''

" They crucified Him.''

" With His stripes we are healed.''

" He was despised and rejected of men.''

" He was wounded for our transgressions.''

" Is it nothing to you, all ye that pass by ?''

" Thou tookest upon Thee to deliver man.''

" He humbled Himself to the death of the Cross.''

" By Thy Cross and Passion, good Lord, deliver us."

" His own self bare our sins in His own body on the tree."

" By Thy precious death and burial, good Lord, deliver us."

TEXTS FOR EASTER.

" He is risen."

" Peace be unto you."

" The Lord is risen indeed."

" King of Kings, Lord of Lords."

" This Jesus hath God raised up."

" Alleluia! Alleluia!! Alleluia!!! "

" I know that my Redeemer liveth."

" Our life is hid with Christ in God."

" Death is swallowed up in victory."

" I am the Resurrection and the Life."

" The Lord is King for ever and ever."

" Death hath no more dominion over Him."

" Christ was raised again for our justification."

" Alleluia! for the Lord God omnipotent reigneth."

" He whom God raised again saw no corruption."

" He is the very Pascal Lamb which was offered for us."

" Thou shalt not suffer Thine Holy One to see corruption."

" This is the Lord's doing, and it is marvellous in our eyes."

" As in Adam all die, even so in Christ shall all be made alive."

" O Death, where is thy sting? O Grave, where is thy victory?"

" Now is Christ risen from the dead, the first-fruits of them that slept."

" Christ our Passover is sacrificed for us, therefore let us keep the feast."

" I am He that liveth and was dead; and, behold, I am alive for evermore."

" Thine eyes shall see the King in His beauty; they shall behold the Land that is very far off."

Texts for Ascension Day.

" Thou art gone up on high."

" He ascended up into Heaven."

" The Lord sitteth a King for ever."

" The Son of Man which is in Heaven."

" Thou sittest at the right hand of God."

" Thou, Lord, art Most High for evermore."

" He ever liveth to make intercession for them."

" From everlasting to everlasting Thou art God."

" Thou hast crowned Him with glory and honour."

" He was taken up, and a cloud received Him out of their sight."

" He was received up into Heaven, and sat on the right hand of God."

Window-Sills.

The decorations suitable for window-sills depend very much on the depth, height, and slope of the sills; some being so high and flat that the surface is hidden from observation, in which case it is useless to decorate more than the front edge with a straight wreath, or with a wreath upon wire which can be bent to any form, such as those shown in Figs. 59 to 62. These, being made of stout wire, may be covered with evergreens interspersed with a few flowers, and tied up with bows or knots of white, yellow, or orange ribbon.

When sloping and in full view, perforated zinc can be cut to the shape and covered with French dried moss, through which and the perforations in the zinc, flowers, either real or artificial, may be thrust. The zinc should be raised a little for this purpose by the insertion of blocks of wood at the corners and the centre. Or the sill may be covered with any red material or paper, and in the centre a painted device may be laid, surrounded by a circular wreath of flowers or variegated evergreen leaves.

Another very pretty method is to cover the sill with damp-proof paper, upon the upper surface of which French moss is to be pasted, if the natural moss cannot be procured, and on this laid garlands of flowers or devices worked in flowers.

Fig. 59.—Festooned Wreath on wire foundation.

These devices may be cut from millboard, as they may be very simple, and the flowers placed upon them. All flowers used should be picked late the day before using, kept in water all night, and placed in position in the early morning; the water absorbed tends to keep them fresh for a consider-able time.

The following combinations will be found effective for

Fig. 60.—Interlaced Wreath on wire foundation.

flower devices, and may be added to indefinitely according to the number and different kinds of flowers available for the purpose :—

1. A *double triangle*, composed of white alyssum and pink azalea. A covering of small green leaves should first be laid over the cardboard foundation, and the white alyssum tacked thickly upon one triangle (care being taken to keep the crossing of the two triangles clear) and the pink azaleas upon

the other.   These two kinds of flowers will keep fresh for a considerable time.

2. A *St. Andrew's Cross* of yellow daffodils or other golden flowers.   The daffodils should, if possible, be the double variety placed singly to form the shape of the cross, and a bright blue ribbon, carelessly but artistically twined round it when finished will look very pretty.

Fig. 61.—Double Festooned Wreath on wire foundation.

3. A *seven-pointed star* of wild blue hyacinths, if the season is late, or the church in the more-favoured Southern counties ; if not, it should be made of greenhouse hyacinths or other blue flowers.   In the centre of the star a knot of narcissi or daffodils may be placed with happy effect.

Fig. 62.—Hanging Device in evergreens and flowers.

4. A *circle of primroses* 2in. or 3in. broad, placed in a circular trough filled with water—as they are very delicate flowers—and set with three or four little bouquets of coloured flowers to form jewels, has a good appearance. Each little bouquet must be of a different kind of flower to give variety—two of blue and two of red flowers should be selected, if they are to be had.

5. *Three circles entwined.* Each circle must be made of a different kind of flower of contrasting colour, selected from azaleas, narcissi, geraniums, white double daisies, blue hyacinths, jonquils, etc.

6. *Crown of five points.* This may be formed of jonquils or celandines, and in the band running round the lower part three or four coloured flowers should be added to represent gems set in little pateræ of fours.

7. A *Maltese Cross* of snowdrops, double white daisies, or double narcissi, with a few jonquils or daffodils as a centre, has a very chaste appearance. A zinc trough made in the form of this peculiar cross and filled with primroses, with a centre of violets, also looks very beautiful.

8. An *anchor* of blue hyacinths, with a rope of yellow flowers wound round it, has a fine effect if placed upon a bed of pressed and dried grasses or leaves.

9. A *heart* of azaleas or geranium blossom, set close together and framed in with dark-leaved ivy upon a pale moss background, has a handsome appearance.

10. The *Sacred Monogram.* The letters " I.H.S." may either be formed into a monogram, with the letters entwining, or each letter placed separately side by side, and surrounded by a circle; or each letter may be made larger and heavier and placed separately direct upon its mossy bed. If the latter mode is chosen, let the centre letter be of scarlet geraniums and the two outer letters of white alyssum; the enclosing circle to be of daffodils or primroses, as in No. 4. Where the letters are laid separately on the background, let the centre one be of azaleas and the other ones of jonquils or white narcissi.

11. A *harp.* The body and upper arm may be made of red geraniums, the pillar of azaleas, and the strings of white immortelles (gnaphaliums) pasted on slips of cardboard and laid in place.

12. *Alpha and Omega.* These two Greek letters (A and Ω) may be made of any kind of flowers available, provided they

are of different kinds.   The letters may be made separately or in the form of a monogram, having daffodils for one letter and double white daisies for the other.   If more colour is required, azaleas and geraniums may be tried, but as Easter is a time of joy as much white as possible should find a place in the decorations.

When natural flowers cannot be obtained for these devices, they may be formed of Cape jasmine, mesembryanthemums, Cape everlastings, fairy flowers, straw, variegated grasses, etc. ; but if real flowers can be obtained they should be used by all means, leaving the dried ones for banners and other purposes.

If texts are preferred to devices on the window-sills, either a very short text must be chosen, complete in itself, or a long text carried right round the church by placing two or three words, in sequence, in each window.   This may be effected by placing a broad strip of some kind of either red or white material, pasted on cardboard, across each sill, thus forming a sequence of labels upon which the letters of the text may be either formed of everlasting flowers or painted on.

Everlastings are now to be bought in a dozen different colours, viz. : white, yellow, red, blue, violet, purple, magenta, green, lilac, pink, solferino, and crimson, so that colours suitable for any kind of background may be selected.

Banners, Shields, &c.

These will find appropriate places upon the wall-spaces between the windows, and on the columns, chancel-screen, or other suitable spots.   They should be suspended, not with invisible wire, which gives a naked, forlorn appearance, but with cord and tassels, which impart a visible means of support and a proper finish.   These cords and tassels should be of the same colour as the background or principal colour used on the banner.   As the banners should bear the devices most appropriate for Easter, we will here give them, adding the details of colouring, &c., afterwards :—

The *Cross of the Resurrection,* or Easter Cross, differs widely from the Greek Cross, and from the Cross of the Passion. The Greek is a poetic idea; the Latin, the instrument of suffering; whilst the Easter Cross is one of triumph, of victory over death and the grave. It may also be used as an Ascension Day decoration. It is different from every other form of cross, being a standard or crosier, and is usually drawn as represented in Fig. 63, having a banner depending from the cross-beam, and bearing the legend or inscription, " Ecce Homo " or " In hoc signo vinces." Sometimes the tall, staff-like cross does not bear either banner or legend, but it s still typical of the Resurrection.

The *Lamb* bearing this cross is another appropriate device, and is one of the most ancient symbols of our Lord. It should bear the sacred nimbus around its head—a white or golden circle with a red cross upon it. The red cross, or red rays, are an especial mark of Divine glory, and if each ray contains a cross emblazoned upon it, it is known as a " cruciferous nimbus." These red rays never appear in the nimbi of saints or angels.

Fig. 63. — Cross and Banner of the Resurrection.

The *Crown of Glory or Victory* is also appropriate. It has a bright star upon each upstanding point, or sometimes the centre point is prolonged and fashioned into a cross fleury. Sometimes it is made to surmount the monogram " I.H.S.," but at other times these letters are thrust through it or sprung from it.

The *Sun* in splendour may also be used as a device, as Easter commemorates the triumph of light over darkness, of life over death.

Other crosses which may be used at this season are the *Cross pattée*, the *Cross fleury*, the *Cross urdée*, and the *Cross pommée*, but it is not advisable to strew crosses indiscriminately all over the church; they should be reserved for the pulpit and chancel. The usual outlines of these crosses are delineated on pages 18 to 21, but for the sake of art treatment or license, they are sometimes drawn with slightly different outlines.

Fig. 64.—Banner emblazoned with the Sacred Monogram.

Banners and shields should not be hung in the chancel, the abode of peace, as they have a certain martial appearance about them.

There is no exact rule as to the shape which either shields or banners may take, but they should be approximately two-thirds as wide as they are high, and the lower portion may be cut to any shape desired, remembering that the "flatiron" shape (Fig. 49) is the oldest form of all. As we have suggested, banners may be of any available material, from painted linoleum or millboard to the richest velvet. Fig. 64 shows one with the sacred monogram upon it as a centre-piece, and with a cross pommée at each corner. The I of the monogram is elongated to form a rayed cross fleury. The groundwork may be in red velvet or rep, the vesica shape which surrounds the letters in moss or fine green leaves of ivy, laurel, or other evergreen, the corner crosses of white wool, and the letters cut from straw tissue, outlined with a deep green line in oil colour.

Another way of working it is as follows :—The letters are formed of plain white cotton-wool on a banner of red flock paper pasted upon millboard to stiffen and preserve it. The pointed oval or vesica may be formed of hyacinths, daffodils, or any other available flowers, and the corner crosses of dried moss,

To show the diversity of material and colouring which may be employed, we give a third way of treating this banner, but with a little trouble or reflection an intelligent worker will be enabled to carry out the execution of this or any other banner in a dozen different ways. Take a piece of linoleum, paint the back a nice soothing, quiet, russet green, and paint the centre portion of the front crimson. Next cut the sacred monogram out of white velvet, and paste accurately in the centre ; round the vesica shape fasten on yellow or white everlasting flowers in a double band, and fill the corners of the banner with grey moss. Add a stick across the back, at the top, then the cord and tassels, and the whole is ready to hang up.

Banners may also be made almost entirely of everlasting flowers, dried French moss, dried grasses, &c.

Straw plaiting of various forms may be used in making devices, and has a good appearance, being raised instead of flat like the straw tissue. It is useful for borders, or for bosses, crosses, trefoils, stars, and other objects.

An attempt has been made to introduce feathers for purposes of decoration, but it is doubtful if this is not rather wide of the general scheme of church decoration, as unusual skill is required to manipulate the feathers so as to present devices at once emblematic and artistic. In expert hands, feathers may be beautifully arranged, but the average church worker will do well to confine himself or herself to the materials in vogue for years past. Feathers of many foreign birds may be bought for the purpose, and those of many

British birds may also be used. Those of the turkey, pheasant, jay, and of the homely rooster, have all been employed, with varying success. Feathers are, however, hardly the " fruit of the earth."

Another simple banner is depicted in Fig. 65—*The Crown of Victory surmounting a Lily.* The background may be of

the palest green material, from wall-paper of a superior kind to the richest grey-moss velvet— according to the funds available. If of the latter material, perhaps some lady-worker will find time to work the crown in gold thread, the lilies in white with gold stamens, and the leaves in varied green silk. If so, the banner will not only serve as an Easter decoration, but will form a permanent addition to the adornments of the church.

Here is a method of making the same banner in a way still more suitable for Easter. Let the ground be of red serge or rep, the crown cut out of straw tissue, with little curved bands of straw piping pasted on, and the lower part studded round with bright-coloured everlasting

Fig. 65.—Fringed Banner with painted and worked Crown and Lily sewn upon it.

flowers as jewels. The markings and detail of the crown may be put in with a camel-hair brush and a little chocolate oil paint. The flowers of the lily should be cut from glossy white linen, and the leaves from green cloth of various colours ; around the edge of the banner straw plait should be sewn, a gold or white fringe being added if desired. The usual stick and a cord and tassels will finish the banner.

The *Lamb bearing a Cross of Victory,* or the Resurrection Cross, may be used as a companion banner. Paint the device on white linen or thin cardboard, and stitch it in the centre of the banner, placing round it a circle of straw tissue, illuminated with a text in red letters with blue capitals. The text should be a short one, such as " The Lord is risen indeed," or " I know that my Redeemer liveth." The edge of the circle may be set round with white immortelles (both the inner and outer circumference), and a neat border of straw plait may be placed round the entire banner.

A *Dove,* formed of the silver leaves of the Cape everlasting, looks well upon a lilac or violet background, and the banner should be bordered with dried white grasses. Little Maltese crosses, cut from silver Cape leaves, may be placed in the corners.

The *Phœnix* is a companion device to the Lamb. The bird may be cut out of straw tissue, and painted in

Fig. 66. — Illuminated Banner of American Cloth with Emblems of the Passion.

oil colour. Round it may be placed a circle of white wool, upon which is arranged a 'little formal wreath of box leaves, set two and two, and beneath it a scroll cut from straw tissue, upon which is painted in red letters, " Alleluia," or " He is Risen." The background may be of red twill or flannel, or of pale blue serge.

Most of the devices may be purchased already outlined, and ready for sewing upon the banner.

ILLUMINATED BANNERS are as simple as any, providing anyone in the congregation, who is an artist, will give his time to painting one or two. Here is the mode of procedure for Fig. 66. Procure a piece of white American cloth, and paste upon the back a piece of red twill, if the banner is to be placed in a position where its back is seen, or if it is to be carried. When dry, cut to the exact shape required, and sew a hem at the top for the stick to pass through. The worker will outline the cross, which should be left white, and colour the four corners yellow (or gold may be used), and upon the background so prepared the various emblems will be painted in their natural colours. The crown of thorns will be painted boldly in brown, and the monogram in red, with a neat black outline to make it legible at a distance. The text, " He is Risen," may be of chocolate letters on a grey-green ground. The banner should be bound with blue silk ribbon or tape, and a gold or blue fringe added.

Where banners are to be at a good distance from the eye a flock paper background may be used, and the devices cut out of straw tissue, gold and silver paper, or white paper, with the emblems painted thereon in either oil or water colours. If oil colours are used the paper or thin cardboard must first be sized.

None of the banners above described are too difficult to be made at home, where they may be taken up at leisure times and put by in readiness for the particular festival for which they are designed.

Devices are sometimes placed upon white walls or *gallery fronts* without any background. These must be fastened to laths or fine wire, and should usually be made of evergreens and everlasting flowers. Leaves do well for the main part of the design, but they should be set off and brightened with bosses of everlasting flowers all of one colour.

The effect of colour depends much upon the distance the object is to be placed from the eye ; thus, a bouquet of taste-fully arranged coloured everlastings will look well when the observer is standing near; but when that bouquet is, say, 30ft., from his eye, it will appear to be a mere jumble of colour, its tasteful arrangement being so blended that it is entirely lost, and the colours neutralised. In such case, therefore, let the bosses be a circle of white, a circle of red, or a knot of yellow everlastings, and the full effect will then remain the same at any distance.

Where the walls of the church are dark in colour, the fine decorative effect of evergreen leaves is mostly lost; therefore, more flowers, natural or artificial, and less leaves, should be employed. The devices should be tied with brightly-coloured ribbons, and the ends allowed to trail down.

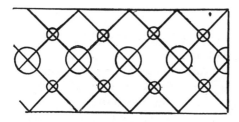

Fig. 67.—Trellis of Deal Laths and circles of Cardboard for Chancel walls.

Large dried white grasses placed in little trophies, or worked into devices, with a few flowers, are also telling on dark walls, and look very graceful.

The Chancel Walls and East Window.

The WALLS OF THE CHANCEL will look well with some pattern of evergreen trellis, such as was mentioned for Christmas (Fig. 34, page 55), or a trellis like that shown in outline in Fig. 67 may be used.

In the first-mentioned, holly must give place to little bosses of bright flowers. In the latter device the small circles may be covered with a large single Fairy flower, and the large circles, painted red, may be encircled with everlastings, or a wreath of jonquils, or be painted with an emblem. Little

H

shields may be hung on them, each bearing a letter to form
a complete text, or any suitable devices.

The sill of the EAST WINDOW—if seen—may be covered
with a mass of flowers, but usually a reredos or curtain hides
it.   In the latter case a handsome Cross of the Resurrection
should be placed in the lower part of the centre light; this
should be formed of white camellias or azaleas pricked into a
bed of wet moss which has been tied to a wooden cross as a
foundation.   The three knobs of the cross, at the extremities
of the arms, may be three red camellias set closely together
on each arm.   Remember to get as much white into the
Easter decorations as possible, as the gloom of Lent has de-
parted, and joy has taken its place.

The Stalls.

These must be fully decorated, and ample has been written
under the head of " Wreaths," " Banners," and " Window-
sills " to furnish material.   The taste of the decorator will suggest the best manner of using them according
to the shape and size of the stalls.   The reader should also
refer to the section on the " Chancel " under " Harvest,"
page 141.

The Communion Table.

Probably the Communion table will be already draped in
white, with permanent flower vases upon it, and, therefore,
will require no more than the ordinary decorations, which are
usually undertaken by the vicar or his wife; but should this
not be the case, a text formed of white flowers may be affixed
either above the table or along its draped front, and stands
of beautiful white flowers may be placed upon the table
itself.

These Easter offerings of flowers are sometimes arranged
in a symbolical manner thus :—Upon a wire stand, which may
be purchased, is arranged a series of little zinc tubes for containing water, the whole stand forming an arc; in the tubes
are arranged a series of flowers to represent a *rainbow*, whilst

in the centre is a tall white cross also of real flowers. This is to typify God's promise and its fulfilment.

Another device, a *Tree of Life rising from a Crown of Righteousness,* may be used; the tree should be a fine branch of real almond blossom, or of blackthorn in full bloom, or if these cannot be procured, a branch from some greenhouse shrub, bearing a wealth of beautiful white blossom, must be substituted. The crown may be formed of yellow flowers, of which several varieties are available at this season. The table should not be crowded, but whatever is placed upon it should be of the best procurable.

The Chancel Screen.

For this it is difficult to lay down any hard-and-fast rules, as but few churches retain their screens, and where they do there are exactly two alike. However, the reader who reads carefully through this Easter section will be at no loss for screen decorations, as any of the wreaths, shields, banners, or devices are at his service, and a little thought will render the mere placing of them an easy task.

The Pulpit and Reading-desk.

PULPITS of coloured marble or granite admit of very little extra colour being introduced; their colouring is already full and bright, and an overloaded appearance is the result of adding more. Where rich carvings are seen, it seems futile to attempt to " gild the lily " by covering decoration with other decoration. Graduated wreaths surrounding the base, composed of fine ivy and ferns, with one or two devices of green and white flowers on red cloth, placed in the panels, will usually be found sufficient.

Where the pulpit is of white stone, a greater display is permissible. A stone pulpit is usually placed upon a massive support, and around its circumference a number of panels are usually cut, or sometimes there are a central column and six or eight minor supports. All these members require decorating, but the base and small pillars only need wreaths of green or grey moss, ferns, dried plants and grasses, &c., and care must be exercised that too much colour is not used for the body of the pulpit, or it will appear top-heavy.

If red is the chief colour employed in the body decoration, then white, yellow, and a little green may be used as supplementary colours. Where blue predominates, white, yellow,

Fig. 68.—Design for decorating a Large Panel in Pulpit, having the "Agnus Dei" emblem in the centre.

and a very little red may be employed in a minor manner. Where white is to be the principal colour, yellow, green, and a little red may be used. Yellow being very bright and prominent in itself, should seldom be used as a chief colour. All the colours except blue may be set off and toned with green, which softens and blends them. Where green is used with blue, great care must be taken that a decidedly yellow tone of green is selected. Attention to these remarks will assure success, where a too liberal mixture of colour will be a certain source of failure.

Pulpits of carved woodwork may be decorated in nearly the same style as stone ones, but should have more white and less yellow upon them, as most woodwork has a yellow tone in itself. The carvings can be emphasised either by placing dark cloth behind any openings in them, or by using box or other leaves, or moss to throw them into relief. When this is done, a paper template of the lower part of the carvings should be cut with scissors, and green moss or leaves pasted upon it before fastening it in place. Box-leaves sewn on a narrow green tape also look well, but the paper will be found easiest and most effectual.

Fig. 68 shows a way of decorating one of the panels of the pulpit, of which there are usually several. The quatrefoil is bordered by a neat evergreen wreath. A different kind of leaf should be used for each medallion or panel round the pulpit, a light and dark one alternately. Then from the four points a thin deal lath should be fixed by notching the ends so as to " spring in " to the space ; these should be covered with red flannel, and upon them a line of ground ivy leaves or any other suitable foliage should be placed, or moss may be used.

In the centre, where the laths cross, a white cardboard disc, with a zig-zag border of red cloth around it, should be placed, and upon the centre should be painted (or one purchased already made) an " Agnus Dei " with a Resurrection Cross. These central devices should be different in each panel, and their colouring should be varied as much as possible. They may contain the Phœnix, sacred monogram, crown and lilies, but the Resurrection Cross should have the place of honour—the centre panel.

Triangles, Maltese and Pommée crosses, circles, and other devices may be placed on beds of moss to fill the corner spandrels. The worker should also refer to page 119.

A circle of scarlet cloth, with one Cape jasmine gummed

upon it, makes a pretty ornament for the corners.   To make
these flowers lie flat and show up well in their star-like
beauty, they should be well warmed in front of a fire, the
centre black spot removed, and then well pressed in a heavy
book.   They are easily pasted to any material, and look well
when placed upside down, that is, with the back upwards.

Where the pulpit has simple, plain panels, or no panels at
all, a device similar to Fig. 69 may be adopted.   It is made

Fig. 69.—Twelve-pointed Star, formed from
four Triangles of Lath.

of four lath triangles, so arranged that with a little manipu-
lation the centre forms a circle.   The laths should be
covered with evergreens, bound on with fine wire in the usual
way, and the circle should then be pricked out with little
bunches of various coloured flowers, while one fine flower
may be placed at each end of the twelve points forming the
star.   The centre circle may be filled with red material, and
upon it affixed the Alpha and Omega device in white and
gold letters.   Or if the evergreens on the triangles be chosen

of a golden hue the centre may be blue, with a large silver crown upon it—or a large golden star, or " I.H.S.," or any other device suitable to Easter, may be placed upon it.

The wreaths of evergreen which are usually placed around the pulpit may be fastened by red ribbons placed in the " cross-garter " fashion seen in architectural " swags " or wreaths. The ends may be allowed to make a negligent flourish.

When two wreaths are used, one at bottom and one at top of the pulpit, the lower one should be thicker than the upper one, and the latter ornamented with azaleas, white primulas, primroses, or other flowers. Some greenhouse flowers last

Fig. 70.—Design for surrounding plain Pulpit or Font with Evergreens on narrow Laths.

better if a drop of gum is dropped into the centre of each petal, as this prevents the petals from falling so soon.

When the body of the pulpit is quite plain, it may be banded round with a device similar to Fig. 70, which is formed of evergreens upon very narrow laths. The whole may be placed upon scarlet cloth, cut in scallops, or " dog-toothed," both at top and bottom. A large Cape flower or any little floral device may be used for the centre of each diamond.

Figs. 71 and 72 show the ground plans of other modes of treating plain surfaces, whether of the pulpit, font, or walls. These are all very simple, but where there are panels in the pulpit, two of the easiest and not the least effective modes of treating them are as follow :—

Cut a paper pattern or shape of the panels to be filled, paste dried moss (or the real moss if it is plentiful in the neighbourhood), upon it, and place upon each panel any device that can be made by unskilled decorators ; even a large, well-arranged bouquet of pale flowers will look well ; in fact, far better than a clumsily-made and ill-proportioned emblem.

The other, and a very simple way is, after cutting out the paper or cardboard shapes of the panels to be decorated, to paste upon them white cotton-wool flatly arranged, and to

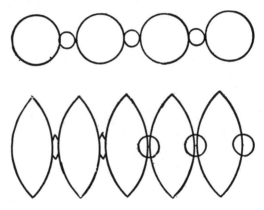

Figs. 71 and 72.—Foundations for Devices for surrounding Pulpit, Font, or Walls.

form a circle, a triangle, and the letters " I.H.S." of leaves or flowers, and place them upon the white background. These devices may be made of natural flowers, interspersed with dried grasses and leaves, or they may be formed of large Cape flowers, with sprays of dried ferns or decorative grass.

Another device easy to make is a large star. Procure a number of immortelles of all colours of yellow from pale lemon to deepest orange, and arrange these by pasting on a cardboard foundation so that the palest are at the points, gradually fastening on those of more positive colour, until at last when the centre is reached, they are of rich orange. The actual centre may be a crimson Cape flower or a boss of blue gnaphaliums (immortelles).

The READING DESK (and the FRONT OF THE ORGAN LOFT, if there is one) must follow the prevailing colours and style of decorations adopted for the pulpit, as given above, but a text and a neatly folded scroll may be added. This should be a short text of victory, such as " Death is swallowed up in victory," and beneath it may hang a couple of shields bearing emblems of the Passion as a remembrance of what our Lord suffered before He gained His glorious victory. They may be painted upon zinc which has been gilded. The various objects depicted may be painted in their natural colours, and rays emanating from them should be blocked in with deep chocolate oil colour, so as to leave the rays to show between the lines of colour. They should not be varnished. When finished the zinc should be slightly bent, like an ordinary defensive shield, as it has a much better effect thus than when perfectly flat.

The Lectern.

This is of various forms, and is either constructed of iron, wood, or brass ; in the last case the devices should be confined to white flowers, green leaves, and a few spots of colour (natural flowers or everlastings). A wreath may be twined round the pillar, having in it any available white flowers, and around the base pots of arum lilies may be placed. The pots may be concealed with moss pasted upon green calico, the mould being covered with sprigs of evergreens or dried ferns, grasses, or moss. Arums are fine decorative flowers and particularly appropriate to Easter. Dried palms or palms in pots will also be found very effective, and as many parts of the world are now scoured to find a supply of these, there is a great choice for the worker. A white velvet or cloth frontal, with a symbol or text embroidered upon it in gold, should be suspended from the desk or eagle.

Gas or Lamp Standards.

A wreath of some kind seems almost self-suggestive. This must not be the somewhat heavy wreath of Christmas, having its deep green hollies and bays set with red berries, but a neat entwining wreath of pale evergreens or dried grasses, set with either real or artificial flowers ; and to give character and set these off, a small shield may be placed on each standard, alternately white and red. A red device on a white shield or a white device on a red shield would form a distinct feature.

If it is desired to have either the backgrounds or the devices of some of these shields of gold this may easily be done thus : cut the shields from millboard, and having melted some house-painter's size by pouring hot water over a little placed in a small cup or pot, brush it over the shield. When quite dry sketch out the device or charge with lead pencil ; whatever parts are to be gilded must then be coated with gold size, which must be watched in drying. When nearly dry— that is, when by placing the tip of the finger upon it a slight stickiness or " tackiness " is felt—it is ready to receive a coating of dry bronze powder, which must be " drifted " upon it and the surplus shaken and brushed off for future use. For this purpose what is known as a " camel-hair flat " should be used because of its softness. Such a brush an inch wide costs sixpence.

If shields are used in the chancel they should be white, with either red, green, or gold devices, or a combination of the three. Usually the standards in the chancel spring from a substantial base, which may be surrounded by pots of arums, red poinsettias, or other flowers, and use may also be made of feathery palms. Uva grass, 5ft. long, is also exceedingly decorative, and not expensive, costing only three or four shillings per dozen. Other very effective dried grasses are *Agrostis nebulosa, Aira pulchella, Briza major* and *B. minor, Lagurus ovatus, Bromus brizæformis,* &c. These are not really expensive, as if they are carefully taken down, dusted, and put away in soft paper, they may be used again and again.

The Font.

For the font, like the pulpit, the scheme of decoration very much depends upon its form and colour, some fonts being almost pure white, whilst others made from slate or Purbeck marble are almost black. It will therefore be seen that there

Fig. 73.—Gothic Arches of stout wire for Font-wreath.

is some difficulty in giving instructions that in all cases shall be helpful; still we will impart a few leading ideas, and leave the worker to select those most appropriate for his particular case.

If deep enough, the body of the font may be embellished with a text running entirely round it, or the space may be occupied by devices fashioned on wires or a kind of trellis work, or shields may be hung round it as in Fig. 49 (p. 71),

Fig. 74.—Wire Foundation for Font-wreath.

or a double wreath twined about it as in Fig. 61 (p. 88). A variation of the groundwork out of the ordinary run is to use a wire frame of Gothic arches, as in Fig. 73. Another device for covering with evergreens and flowers, to be placed upon a font with an unornamented bowl, is given in Fig. 74.

It makes a great difference whether the cover of the font is removed or retained in its place, as in the former case natural flowers find no support, except on the rim or when floating on the water with which the font is at such times filled.

When the cover is allowed to remain on, if it should be a tall, pointed one a pretty decoration is to cover it with white frosted wool, and then entwine it with a long garland of flowers set upon a leafy background. Grasses of various kinds may encircle the base of the cover.

Another plan is to divide it into six or eight compartments, and to cover each of these sections with pale evergreens and flowers alternately, or each division may be blazoned with a different kind of flower set upon an evergreen or moss background. The top may be encircled with a crown of white camellias, girded around with a belt of yellow flowers.

If the font-cover is removed, any appropriate device may be floated upon the water by inserting cut flowers into one of the numerous patterns of zinc troughs made for the purpose. In this case the edge of the font will require a fine garland of flowers made to the exact width of the rim laid upon it, and from it pretty trailing sprays of ivy may depend.

To cover the body of a very plain font, sew a broad band of red cloth round it and form a text upon it in everlasting flowers ; such a text as " One Law, one Faith, one Baptism," " Suffer Little Children to come unto Me," or " Repent, and be Baptised," will be of sufficient length if the letters are made fairly large, and a little border of single leaves of golden laurel placed so that they overlap each other will make a neat finish.

Where a change from the above is required, the following plan may be tried with any variations that suggest themselves according to the shape of the font :—At equal intervals around the font place small red shields having white devices upon them, and link them together with little garlands of flowers and foliage.

Sometimes the verge of the font is covered with moss, with a few choice flowers laid upon it, and although the season is early, yet there are many flowers to select from, among them being azaleas, hyacinths, jonquils, daffodils, camellias, geraniums, cyclamens, deutzias, primulas, primroses, celandine, narcissi, poinsettias, forget-me-nots, and many others.

In ornamenting the pillars of a font that are not wholly detached from the central column it is often found difficult to attach the wreaths, as nails cannot be used for fixing them, and it is impossible to tie them; but the difficulty may be overcome by using stout wire as a foundation, and bending the wire to the shape of the pillar during the process of making up. The wire will act as a kind of spring, and when placed upon the half-pillar will cling to it and retain its position.

One of the chief aims of the church decorator should be to convey to the congregation the reasons for the various decorations; therefore, different devices are considered appropriate and reserved for the different seasons and festivals of the year, and also for particular saints, whether patron or otherwise. To aid this differentiation colour has been invoked, and to some purpose when properly used. As symbolism and colouring have each their proper place in church work, it is not only bad taste, but shows ignorance of simple rules to display either wrong colours or emblems, such as the devices for Whitsuntide, at Christmas, or the emblem of one saint as that of another. It will be very helpful to decorators if they will read the sections on " Christmas," " Whitsuntide," and " Harvest," each of which gives many hints applicable to general decoration at all seasons.

Whitsuntide.

ALTHOUGH Whitsuntide is one of the four great festivals when church decorations are most in vogue, it certainly has not the same deep, sympathetic hold on Christian congregations as those of Christmas, Eastertide, and Harvest. Pentecost was a Jewish festival, therefore is of much more ancient origin than any Christian festival. As its name (from Greek *pentekoste*, fiftieth) denotes, it was held fifty days after the feast of Unleavened Bread. As a Christian festival its interest arises from its being the day upon which the Holy Ghost descended upon the Apostles in the form of tongues of flame, imparting to every man the gift of speech in foreign languages.

It is a remarkable fact that this feast does not appear to have had even a name in the early centuries of the Western Church, yet we know that in Western Europe Pentecost was a time of great rejoicing, and was considered a day of more importance than can be easily explained by the incidents connected with it, as recorded in the Gospels, or from any later legends attached to it. In mediæval times it was one of the great festivals of kings and princes, as those who have read Malory's " Morte d'Arthur " will remember. At any rate, the Christian Pentecost (now more generally known as Whitsuntide), in Western Europe at least, has been and is regarded as one of the chief festive periods of the year. With its feasts and Whitsun ale and Morris dances we have nothing to do. We only regard it in its sacred aspect of a

Church festival, in its connection with Holy Writ, though we know that the " rites "of mediæval days were principally paid for by the churchwardens of the various parishes, and that the mummery which took place at Whitsuntide was no credit to the Church.

Some of the ancient " churchwardens' accounts " point to Whitsun as being a time of church decoration. In Elizabethan days we find in the accounts of St. Mary-at-Hill, London, the following entry : " Garlands, Whitsunday, iijd." Some three hundred years ago one John Lane, of Yatton, in Somerset, left half an acre of land called the " Groyes " to the poor for ever, the grass from which was " for strewing of the Parish Church on Whitsunday."

In Whitsuntide decoration we must remember that it is the period dedicated to the Holy Ghost, which, in the form of a Dove, descended upon the Apostles after the Ascension of our Lord. A cloven tongue of fire rested above each one's head as an outward and visible sign.

Banners and Devices.

Bearing in mind the above facts, we must adopt for our principal banners and devices symbols set apart for the Third Person of the Trinity, the Holy Ghost. The devices used to denote God the Father, God the Son, and God the Holy Ghost are all appropriate, but none of those which commemorate the Virgin Mary or the Saints should be used. The principal devices of the Holy Ghost are the Dove, the Aureole of Seven Circles, the Tongues of Flame, the Twelve Suns and Twelve Stars, the Nine-pointed Star, the Six-pointed Star, and the Cross of Iona. These we will examine more in detail.

The *Dove* (Fig. 75) must be of white or silver, and represented in the act of flying as if descending from Heaven upon the Apostles. A very realistic effect is produced by suspending an artificial dove from the roof of the chancel, so that it hangs about 9ft. from the ground, but to make it visible in the body of the church it must be greatly exaggerated in size. The dove may be modelled in clay or neatly carved in wood, the body being of one piece and the wings of two other pieces, which after carving may be attached to the body. It should then be painted white. The nimbus may be of cardboard covered with gold paper upon which a red cross is painted. Some go so far as to seek the aid of the bird-stuffer to cover the large model with feathers neatly glued on.

Around the Dove, to complete the emblem, a large iron hoop should be suspended, after being first gilded. Around the hoop stout pieces of paper must be glued, jutting outward and downward, to represent the tongues of flame. They

Fig. 75.—The Dove—Represented as if Descending from Heaven.

should also be gold, of a cloven form, and touched with red paint to represent flame. In ancient times the tongues were frequently formed in the shape of the human tongue—the tongue of language rather than that of flame.

The *Aureole of Seven Circles* (Fig. 76) should be yellow and white. When the little celandine is still available it is very suitable to form the seven circles. It should be gathered a week or two before it is wanted, and pressed between heavy books; it will then last much longer than when freshly gathered. The circles should first be carefully covered with moss and the celandine flowers afterwards added. These little flowers may occupy four circles, whilst the remaining three may be covered with narcissi, with their white, star-like petals. A single row of each flower will be ample.

The *Tongues of Flame* are used where a background of some kind is available. They may be cut from the best gold paper, or if the metallic or tinselly appearance is objected to, any thin paper may be gilded with ordinary transferred gold leaf. In either case the tongues, which should be cloven, may be tipped with vermilion paint, vivid at the points and merging gradually into the gold the further it recedes from the points. The aim is to obtain the appearance of a bright jet or tongue of flame.

The *Twelve Suns* and *Twelve Stars* (Fig. 77), too, are only applicable to devices which have a background. As

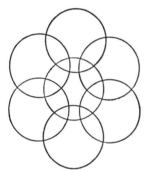

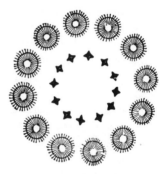

Fig. 76.—Aureole of Seven Circles, to be carried out in Yellow and White.

Fig. 77.—Twelve Suns and Twelve Stars for Device on a Banner or Shield.

a banner, the device may be arranged thus : The background should be blue, leaning to the light rather than to the dark side, the suns being of gold, and the stars of silver. If the devices are to be in flowers, a large circle must first be struck with a pair of compasses, and the circle divided into twelve (half the radius), each of the twelve divisions having a sun placed upon it. Within this circle of suns a smaller circle must be struck, and also divided into twelve portions, on each of which a silver star must be fastened. The suns may be circles of thin cardboard, with gilded surface of paper attached, the rays being formed by " cutting in " the blue

I

colour of the background so as to form the rays. This is done by pasting the circles upon the background in their correct positions, and then forming small rays by paint of the exact shade of the backgrounds. The silver stars may be made by cutting them from silver paper. A well-defined star should be cut out in cardboard and used as a pattern to pencil round for the other stars. The suns may be cut with a pair of scissors from gold paper—simply circles neatly indented all round with wavy rays to represent " the sun in splendour."

The suns and stars will be almost too small to be worked in flowers without looking clumsy; but if it is thought necessary, they may be used thus : cut the suns, with their rays, from gold paper, and upon the centre of each paste a large golden-dyed fairy flower. For the stars a single pure white everlasting flower may be attached to the centre of each.

As a finish, the corners of the banners may be embellished with a spray of natural flowers placed on at the last moment. For this purpose use the beautiful white narcissi, Star of Bethlehem, jonquils, or lilies of the valley.

The *Nine-Pointed Star* is indicative of the results of the gifts of the Holy Spirit, namely,—Faith, Love, Long-suffering, Gentleness, Goodness, Joy, Meekness, Peace, and Temperance. Each point represents one of these blessings, and the whole star may be made of small flowers, care being taken that a different flower is used for each ray, or that the colours of the flowers are kept separate from each other, so that no two neighbouring colours shall be alike. The points of the star must be coloured thus :—Two white, two blue, two yellow, and three red. The star may be either of wood or perforated zinc painted green; if of wood, it must be bored full of small holes; the zinc is already bored. Before placing the flowers in position, which must be done as late as possible, a thick backing of cotton-wool should be placed on the star, so that when the stems are thrust through the holes, they will pass through and be held by it. This may then be kept saturated with water to preserve the flowers.

Another plan is to form the entire star of blue, red, white, and yellow everlasting flowers, pasted upon a millboard background.

If the star is cut from a half-inch board, it may be covered with the everlastings advised above, with the addition of a row of box or other small leaves pasted to the periphery of the board all round, so as to cover the unsightly wood and the outer flowers, and yet to stand above them and make a thin green framing.

The *Six-Pointed Star*, being the emblem of Creation, is also appropriate to Whitsuntide, and may be made in a similar way and with similar materials to the Nine-Pointed Star.

The *Cross of Iona*, or *Irish Cross*, is well adapted for flower decoration, hyacinths showing to great advantage upon it. The body of the cross should be of white hyacinths, with a centre of blue, and the circle embracing

Fig. 78.—Cross of Iona, or Irish Cross, of Immortelles and Cape Flowers.

the limbs of pink ones of the palest shade.

A very pretty cross may also be made either of natural flowers or of everlasting flowers of different sizes. Fig. 78 is one of the latter. The cross is of wood, and is so simple that any handy person can make it with a couple of lengths of half inch or three-quarter inch deal and four screws. It should be covered with white swansdown (or if too expensive, with serge or nuns cloth) stretched over the front and edges of the cross, and secured at the back with short tinned tacks, so that they are easy of removal. All round the margin of the cross a single row of pink immortelles (a mere flesh colour) should be pasted. Next five fine fairy flowers should be fastened where shown. The centre should be formed by a large Cape everlasting pasted on back upward, and surrounded by rays of the silver Cape leaves which have such a beautiful flossy, velvety appearance. The large circle may be of small Cape leaves, with a little knot of very pale everlastings in the centre of each curved piece. The colouring may be changed in many ways, being a matter of taste, but in any case white, the colour for Whitsuntide, should predominate, and the other colours should be mere *shades*, not positive colour, or the delicacy of the whole device will be spoiled.

The Cross upon the Communion Table, which since Easter has been the Resurrection Cross, should now be removed, and that of the *Atonement* put in its place. This cross is upon three steps representing Faith, Hope, and Charity. The lower one is chosen to represent Charity or Love as it rests upon earth, love being the one virtue which unites earthly joys with hopes of heaven. Hope, the middle step, rests upon love; and Faith, the top step, supports the cross, without which both hope and love would merely be human virtues.

This cross, being a temporary one, may be made of wood painted green, and the flowers bound on with wire; or the cross may be covered with a loose woolly cloth upon which the flowers may be sewn; small ferns and grasses may be interspersed with the flowers.

A splendid cross may be made of white azaleas or the beautiful heads of white rhododendrons set off with fern sprays. If these large flowers are used for the cross, a series of zinc water tubes may be fastened to the wooden cross for holding them, or a zinc trough cross made with a series of water receptacles or pockets may be used. Such a device costs, for one standing 24in. high, about 15s., and many other devices in zinc for keeping cut flowers in fresh condition may be had at proportionate prices from Messrs. Cox, Sons, Buckley and Co., 10, Henrietta Street, Covent Garden, W.C.

The steps of a zinc cross are also receptacles to hold water, so that there is no more trouble required than to arrange the flowers in them. The flowers for the lower step should be pansies, as they are emblematic of Charity. Hope should be typified by blue flowers such as forget-me-nots or hyacinths; Faith is represented by red flowers, of which at this time of year there is an abundance. Geraniums are now plentiful, and make a good decorative bloom, being short, and, when arranged in masses, a capital foil to white flowers.

White lilac for decoration should be more used than it is, especially where large masses of colour are required. A wreath of it placed on a bedding of its own leaves makes a very handsome decoration for Communion rails, pulpit, screen, or reading desk. The only objection to lilac leaves is that they will not last more than a day, but by the end of May there is plenty of foliage of other flowers to select from, such as hardy and greenhouse ferns or arbor vitæ.

In choosing the ferns, those having most seeds upon them should be preferred, as they will retain their freshness longest; being the oldest of the leaves they are darker than the young fronds, but that only adds to their effectiveness as a background for any pale flowers. Ferns grown in a hot-house are of very little use, as they quickly lose their beauty of form and freshness. Before using ferns, immerse them in water for half an hour or so; the moisture they imbibe will then keep them for a long time in good condition.

The outdoor hyacinth is one of the best flowers for retaining its freshness, its thick, tuberous stem storing a large amount of moisture.

The cut flowers should be stood in a bowl of water for two or three hours before being used.

The rhododendron is a robust flower and looks very beautiful when placed in large masses round or upon the font, or round the base of either pulpit or reading desk. Where it is plentiful it looks well laid on the window sills upon a bed of foliage.

May—the hawthorn blossom—is useless, as it fades almost immediately, but the season being one full of fragrant flowers, there is never any difficulty in procuring large quantities of bloom, both from hall and cottage.

Judgment should be used in keeping Whitsuntide quite free from any semblance to Christmas or Easter, both in floral and foliated decorations.

Texts.

Of these there is not a great selection, as Whitsuntide does not approach in importance the festivals of Christmas and Easter.

Texts for Whitsuntide.

" Veni, Creator, Spiritus."

" Baptized with the Holy Ghost."

" The Comforter which is the Holy Ghost."

" They were all filled with the Holy Ghost."

" The Holy Ghost, the Lord and Giver of Life."

" The Spirit beareth witness because the Spirit is Truth."

" The Holy Ghost fell upon them that heard the Word."

" The Holy Ghost came down at this time from Heaven."

" I will pray the Father, and He shall give you another Comforter."

" Thou only, O Christ, with the Holy Ghost, art most high in the glory of God the Father."

Texts for Trinity Sunday.

" Not three Gods, but one God."

" God anointed Jesus of Nazareth with the Holy Ghost."

" The Father is God, the Son is God, the Holy Ghost is God."

" Glory be to the Father, and to the Son, and to the Holy Ghost."

" O Holy, blessed, and glorious Trinity, three persons and one God."

" Holy, Holy, Holy, Lord God Almighty, which was, and is, and is to come."

The texts chosen for Whitsuntide may be affixed upon the usual deal frames, facilities for making which have been enhanced by the introduction of zinc and iron corner clips, so made that by placing them over the corners of the four pieces of deal forming the framing, and driving in a few screws, they are ready for stretching the ground-work of calico or serge over.

Whichever of the numerous materials spoken of in the previous sections is chosen for background, a text of natural flowers may be placed and fastened through by means of a needle threaded with fine wire. Leaves may also be used to throw into relief, or to relieve the monotony of too many, flowers. Of course, the colour of the flowers must be dominated by the colour of the background chosen, and a contrast of colour observed, or the letters at a short distance will appear to mingle with the background and be unintelligible. For this reason white flowers on a red ground or red flowers on a white ground will look well. If blue flowers are chosen, a beautiful background may be formed by pasting straw tissue over the common calico stretched upon the frame. A border of pale green leaves will look well on background of any colour. Remember the rule : letters half the height of the background.

The Pulpit.

The pulpit panels may be filled with demi-angels, that is cut off below the waist, and holding in their hands emblems upon shields, such as those shown in Figs. 79 to 81. These

Fig. 79.

Fig. 80.

Fig. 81.

DESIGNS OF DEMI-ANGELS, HOLDING SHIELDS, to be painted on Canvas or Linoleum for Pulpit Panels.
The "C" in Fig. 80 is the ancient form of "S."

should be sketched in pencil upon stout cartoon paper and coloured *very* boldly in water-colours, giving firm thick out-lines of sepia or deep chocolate colour. The figures should be solely of white and gold, with little peeps of red back-ground to throw them into relief. A single line of pale blue or green everlasting flowers may serve as a border and to hide any little defects in fitting the paper in its appointed panel. Thin millboard will, perhaps, do better than car-toon paper, only it is too absorbent to take colour properly ; if it is used it must have a facing of good cartridge or Whatman's N.H.P. paper pasted over it.

Unless the angels are boldly and broadly drawn, they will look from a distance only like blots of dirty white paper, and unless they are well drawn they are better omitted, as the pulpit is no place for amateur experiments or caricatures.

Any symbols appropriate to the festival may be placed on the shields, or each shield may be charged with a little bouquet of flowers, such as we recommended for the steps of the cross, viz., the pansy, the forget-me-not, and the red geranium. To these may be added other emblematic flowers dedicated to the Saviour, lilies of the valley, star of Bethle-hem, the guelder rose, white rose, and others. Little bou-quets of any of these flowers pinned upon the shields, in zinc water tubes, make a unique device, and they may be changed daily for fresh ones.

When simple little floral devices are only meant to last for a day, cut the ground out of cardboard, and upon it paste small flowers and leaves, seeing that flat flowers, or those by nature adapted for the purpose are selected. The flowers chosen should be single ones—that is not the convoluted double varieties—flat, rather than upstanding or cup-like, and short petalled. The scarlet geranium is a good type, as it is easily opened and pressed flat for sticking on the desired device. Alyssum for white flowers and furze blossom or broom (laid on sideways) for yellow flowers, both lend themselves to this kind of work. Whatever flowers are chosen, they should be gently pressed before they are pasted on; if they will not press flat they are difficult to handle, and others should be sought to take their place.

Chancel-walls and Window-spaces.

For chancel wall-decoration some kind of trellised wreath work will be found most effective. The trellis-work must

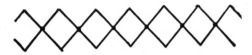

Fig. 82.—Square-on-edge pattern for Evergreens.

be narrow, or it will look very clumsy. It may be formed of laurustinus or the long runners of ground ivy, which are easier to make up than any other evergreen, because they only need a tie here and there. If the latter is used it should have little bunches of red, white, and blue flowers inserted at intervals.

Fig. 62 (p. 88) worked on wire, and with two quite different coloured kinds of leaves, will look well if placed several

Fig. 83.—Simple Trellis of Deal Laths for Evergreens.

feet from the floor. As a change, this pattern, if you have preserved the wire foundation, might be worked upside down to give a " bower-like " instead of a " festooned " effect. The straight heavy wreath may be of laurel leaves bound to a piece of deal an inch square, through which the wires are inserted. The arches may be of arbor vitæ and the diverging upright sprays of yew. Handsome bosses of rhododendrons or roses may be placed where shown, and little sprigs of yew fastened to wires may depend from the main wreath and break its monotonous straightness. Other colourings may be adapted to the taste of the worker.

A much simpler but very effective device may be made on the ground plan shown in Fig. 82—a square-on-edge device of narrow deal laths tied together at the dots, or a single

Fig. 84.—Device made with leaves of Ivy, Yew, &c., and with Everlasting Flowers.

screw will answer the same purpose. It will be observed that the device resolves itself into two zig-zags crossing each other, and these look exceedingly well if one is made of pale but bright evergreens, and the other of flowers with a few little sprays of fern or other foliage showing at intervals. If flowers are not available, two kinds of leaves may be used, and a bow of coloured ribbon or a rosette placed at the crossing of the trellis.

An even simpler device is shown at Fig. 83. A foundation of deal laths should be fastened with screws at the black dots. Upon the trellis thus formed fine strands of ground ivy or other evergreens should be wired, and where the laths cross each other at the dots, a little bunch of bright flowers should be fastened; these latter, if wished, may be renewed occasionally, or a zinc water tube may be fastened at each of the points, and freshly-cut flowers inserted in them. Many villagers will look upon a daily replenishing of these flowers as a privilege and a labour of love.

A fine large device for placing on the blank spaces between windows may be made as follows:—Prepare a double triangle of deal laths to represent the Creator of the Elements and the Trinity with their perfect equality and unity (Fig. 84). The ivy leaves on one triangle should be selected for their large size and fastened on singly, overlapping each other as shown. The other triangle may be covered with yew or any other leaves of a distinctly different type and colour from the ivy. The Crown in the centre with its rays represents the Majesty and Glory of the Trinity. To frame the rays a circle of everlasting flowers—representing eternity—should be fastened, and beyond them a row of fine shimmery Cape leaves may be added. Instead of the Crown and rays for the centre, a double six-pointed star may be used. This symbolises the Creator and was anciently used to represent fire and water.

The Font.

Floral decorations for the font are at this season peculiarly appropriate, and ropes of roses form very beautiful objects for its adornment. Possibly the church may possess one of the large crown-like wire font-cover frames, some of which are set with little tubes for holding water. If not, one may be had 3ft. high for about 14s., or 4ft. high for 18s., from

Messrs. Cox, Sons, Buckley and Co., Henrietta Street, Covent Garden, W.C., and such frames save a very great amount of trouble. One of these should be treated thus :— Wreath the curved uprights with white roses and insert coloured roses in the tubes, finishing the apex with a fine bouquet of cut flowers. From the edge of the rim of the font hang ropes of roses to the floor. The number of the ropes must depend on the shape and size of the font. If it is octagonal, use eight ropes, one from each angle; if it is round, use any number from six to a dozen.

To fasten the lower ends to the floor, so that the garlands or ropes of roses hang in graceful curves, adopt the follow-ing plan. Procure some clay and knead it well, forming it into a number of large balls equal to the number of garlands. Press the balls until they become of the shape of a hemisphere. In these make a number of deep holes with a blunt pointed stick, and nearly fill the holes with water, into which cut flowers may be thrust. These clay receptacles being very heavy, will act as weights on the ends of the garlands to keep them in place. Finally they should be covered with bright green natural moss between the stems of the flowers, or the moss may be put on before the holes are made, in which case care is required not to disarrange it. Round the base of the font pots of fine flowers may be placed and the pots hidden in evergreens, which will act as a splendid foil to the roses and other flowers.

As devices and symbols will be used in other parts of the church, it will be as well to avoid employing any on the font.

The Pillars, etc.

For hints on garnishing the pillars and other parts not specially dealt with under " Whitsuntide," the decorator should consult the sections on " Christmas," " Easter," and " Harvest," as much of the information there given may be adapted to this festival.

Harvest.

THE thanksgiving for harvest is undoubtedly the oldest of all feasts, and was indeed an institution among the people of Israel. As they were a pastoral people, whose wealth consisted of their lands and flocks, it was of vital import- ance to them that their energies and thoughts should be directed to the cultivation and improvement of their land, so that their harvest should be abundant. To this end Moses, the great law-giver, minutely instructed them, not only as to the religion which was to be their guide through life, but also as to the proper times and modes of sowing and reaping, justly reasoning that the best way of rendering that religion understood and appreciated by the uneducated masses, was to connect it closely with the labours of their daily life.

The Jews, on the gathering of any crops, at whatever time of the year, were commanded to give a tithe of it unto the Lord, in appreciation of the blessings bestowed upon them, and of the three great festivals of the Jewish year, two were to be acknowledgments of the bountifulness of God. The first of these was observed at the opening of harvest, the first sheaf reaped being carried to the Temple, and offered to the Lord by the priest, before which dedication no person was allowed to eat either green corn or bread made from the new corn. Seven weeks after this ceremony the second and great festival was celebrated, the people being instructed thus :—"And ye shall take you on the first day the boughs of goodly trees, branches of palm trees, and the boughs of thick trees, and willows of the brook; and ye shall rejoice before the Lord your God seven days. . . . It shall be a statute *for ever* in your generations; ye shall celebrate it in the seventh month." (Leviticus xxiii. 40-41). In Isaiah lx. 13, we find these words pointing to the decoration of God's house :—" The glory of Lebanon shall come unto thee, the fir tree, the pine tree, and the box together, to beautify the place of My sanctuary."

The same feeling of gratitude in man towards his God beat in the breasts of the Egyptians long before the days of Moses, for they made offerings of corn and flowers to Isis. Later the Romans decorated the temples of Ceres, and, indeed, both these gods are frequently represented crowned with corn.

We find similar customs among the early Christians, but gradually it lost its sacred significance, and in mediæval times it degenerated into " Harvest Home," a time of merriment, dancing, and drunkenness. Happily this custom has gradually died out, and the Harvest Thanksgiving is again taking its place as a sacred festival.

Before the " harvest frolic " died, another old custom was practically given up; that of strewing churches with rushes. The rushes, the sweet smelling *Acorus Calamus*, were once strewn in most of our country churches, but it is doubtful if a single church at the present day carries out the custom, though it lingered till recent times in some parts of Cheshire and Lincolnshire. At two or three churches the aisles are still strewn with grass or hay.

Before commencing the actual work of decorating for a Harvest Festival, it is a good plan to ascertain, as far as possible, what fruits, flowers, and evergreens are obtainable, so that a plan of decoration may be formed before any work is begun. From the nature of the materials the work must be carried out as expeditiously as possible, and much time is lost if no pre-conceived plan is decided upon. All the wooden frames may be made in advance—frames for chancel screen (if there is no permanent one), for window ledges, devices, trellis work, and texts. Later the evergreen wreaths may be prepared, and finally the wealth of fruit and flowers added.

The farmers supplying the corn should send it in neatly tied sheaves, straight from the fields, so that the straw remains undamaged. The village children may be set to gather wild berries and tie them in bunches, so as to be ready to hand, and the wreaths of various leaves, sprigs, and sprays may be prepared. Texts of leaves or flowers may have the backgrounds placed on the frames, or if the texts are to be illuminated they may be finished and stood aside. Banners may be prepared ready for the reception of flower and leaf borders, and bulrushes, water-lilies, grasses, coloured bracken, &c., collected.

If all these items are attended to in advance, there will be the more time to spend upon the decoration day, and the appearance of the church will be far finer than when everything has been left for a final rush—when things must be left as placed, without any time being allowed for alterations or improvements.

The finest fruits and the rarest flowers must be reserved for the chancel and the east end of the nave. The pillar wreaths require bold flowers and combinations; the window sills and minor walls need not be too elaborate; but the pulpit, reading-desk, font, and chancel screen must be reserved for the best workers, and great attention must also be given to the chancel itself.

All kinds of fruits and flowers and also vegetables are admissible, but the less decorative of the last-named may be assigned back places. There is not much artistic effect to be obtained from a red cabbage or a giant potato, although they have as much claim to be represented as the finest hot-house grapes, and the refusal of such vegetables is a double rebuff to the poor; it checks the willing and thankful giver, and prevents the receiver from benefiting from what he may actually need. As a country vicar once remarked to the writer, " I bar nothing; potatoes and cabbages may come by the cartload, and what I cannot exhibit I can store. The greater my store, the better for the deserving poor of my parish, and they are many." This may be a useful hint to others who do not mind a little trouble.

Apples, pears, plums, grapes, and in fact almost every kind of fruit may be worked into devices with happy results, and so also may some of the vegetables, such as gourds of all shapes, beets, custard marrows, cucumbers, and others. Barley, wheat, oats, and rye, berries, flowers, and autumn-tinted leaves are all in great request, and when grasses, ferns, and bracken are added, a wonderful wealth of decorative material will be at command.

The best leaves to use are those of the Virginia and Veitch's creepers, the lance-like cherry leaves, the copper beech, the yellow leaves of the golden laurel, the mountain ash, the fading bracken, asparagus, tops of carrots, feverfew, and others.

The symbolical colours for the festival—red, blue, and yellow—are easily represented by berries, flowers, and corn. They could be worked out exceedingly well in poppies, corn-flowers, and king-cups, but such flowers are useless for the purpose, dying almost before they have been assigned to their places. Scarlet geraniums, blue agapanthus, lilies, and marigolds will, however, be found to answer the conditions required very effectively.

Some of the fruits have symbolic meanings, but not many. A cluster of *grapes* is an emblem of our Lord, a type of the blood He shed for us. Grapes also signify abundance. The vine is dedicated to God as a symbol of the power of His Gospel, spreading forth its roots and branches in all directions. *Wheat*, the foundation of bread, represents the staff of life. The *apple* is typical of the fall of man, but when held in Christ's hand is typical of victory over sin.

K

The *pomegranate*, closed, represents majesty from the little crown on the apex, but when bursting open, showing the seeds, is emblematic of life and immortality, as the seed of the plant typifies the continuance of life. The *fig* represents long life, endurance. The symbolic meaning of some of the flowers used we have mentioned on page 22.

Window-sills.

These can be arranged in many ways, according to their depth, number, &c. A simple but effective plan is to fill them with bracken, the greater part green, but with some beautiful fading specimens judiciously placed here and there. When many red and yellow fronds are used, scarcely anything else is required; but if fruit is plentiful, pretty little osier baskets may be suspended from a garland hanging low across the window, each filled with moss, dried grasses, and fruit. Wire stands are now sold for the purpose of containing little trophies of fruit and flowers, and as they raise the objects from the level of the sill into a pyramidal grouping they are to be recommended.

Another plan is to have an arch of wire or sapling ash standing in each window. The ends of the wire or sapling are tied to a lath and thrust against the window jambs, and a wire or string leading to the base of the window holds it in place, leaning a little forward.

A fine trailer of Virginia creeper may be twined round the arches, or a different kind of leaf may be used for the various arches, so as to give variety; thus others may be clad in hop-bine, ivy, clematis, Passion flower, and so on. Clusters of nuts may be introduced upon little branches still retaining their leaves. The black bryony with its clusters of red and green berries is also a very decorative plant, but unfortunately the leaves fade quickly. Then we have the fruit-bearing laurel (*Aucuba*) with its clusters of sable berries, the scarlet barberry, used with ivy leaves, as its own fade rapidly, the berries of the mountain ash, small

outdoor grape leaves, and many more. Oak leaves, copper
beech leaves, and many others may be made much use of.

Heather and ling, sweet-smelling and effective, make
capital covering for window-sills, and little sheaves or
devices of corn laid upon it have a pretty appearance. A
St. Andrew's cross, formed in four different windows, of
wheat, barley, rye, and oats laid upon a bed of green bracken,
looks well. Where the four arms meet, a boss of bright
flowers (red or blue for choice)
should be placed. Simple circles of
various coloured flowers may alternate with the crosses, which may
also be of the Maltese form.

Lilies of various colours —red,
white, blue, and yellow—are to be
obtained, and should be made much
of ; the same may be said of dahlias,
both the single and double varieties.

Plain wooden crosses covered with
moss and then set with China asters
are easy to make, and are uncom-
mon. Fig. 85 is a cross of unusual
design, but is simply a deal cross with
coarse canvas stretched over it and
tacked at the back. Upon this is a
central device on millboard, a facing

Fig. 85.—Cross made upon
Wooden Frame with
Device bearing Sacred
Monogram.

of straws being pasted upon it. The straws are not flat like straw-
tissue, but little lengths of round oat straw, which is brighter
and more golden than that of other corn. Upon this in everlasting flowers, dyed red, the sacred monogram is worked,
and round the edge is fastened a border of bright green moss.
The arms of the cross are bordered with evergreen leaves,
set down the centre with small dahlias, either white or yellow,
and little clusters of three double red dahlias finish the ends.

When fruit is placed on the window-sills, let it be with
method. One would not expect fruit to be brought to table

in chaotic abundance, nor may it be dumped upon a window-sill without some effort of order and forethought. Wire stands are now to be had at a cheap rate, which form capital aids to the display of fine rosy apples, russet pears, and rubicund tomatoes. Beets and carrots, with their feathery heads, may be arranged round the stands and veiled and set out with other fruits, grasses, and asparagus heads. Some fruit may grace the arches spoken of on page 122, and some may have trailing sprays of ivy suspended from them.

Ivy being always in season, its beautifully-shaped and fine glossy leaves, and its bunches of berries, have always been useful. The Druids of ancient Britain and the mystic mistletoe were inseparable, and so too were the followers of Bacchus, the old Roman god, and the ivy with garlands of which they decorated themselves; but for some occult reason the mistletoe is discarded and the ivy retained—why, it would be difficult to say, but modern decorators should be thankful that the useful ivy, rather than the mistletoe, is still allowable in churches.

Where pyramids of fruit and vegetables are used, the coarser kinds should form the base—the potatoes and carrots alternating in a circle covered with leaves, then should come small gourds and cucumbers, more leaves, then fruit, still more leaves, and then an apex of fruit and flowers. In the interstices of the layers sprays of fern, carrot top, asparagus top, grasses, &c., will give a feathery, indefinite outline to the group. Grey ash leaves look well as a contrast to the golden and ruddy glow of the fruit.

The Pillars.

These look well when entwined with hop-bines. A broad band of blue or red flannel, scalloped at the bottom, may be placed immediately beneath the capital, the colours running alternately, and upon this may be shown little sheaves of grain of any kind with fruit hanging between, or little bunches of coloured flowers may take the place of fruit, and so be less likely to lead little hands into temptation. Apples caused the fall of man : boys are not immune! A wreath of red dahlias on a background of green calico, zigzagged at the bottom, looks well if placed just below the capital. Asters may be placed on every other column, or various coloured dahlias may grace the different columns. Where the columns are very bulky a festooned wreath with trailing sprays of ivy or other creeping plant, as shown in Fig. 86, may be fastened round the upper part of the shaft.

For the lower parts of the columns, resting upon the base, ordinary green wreaths without flowers may be placed ; that

Fig. 86.—Suggestion for a Wreath to encircle the upper part of the Shaft of a Pillar.

is, if they will be seen. If the columns are set round with pillars, rods or laths may be covered with leaves and stood in the upright hollows. If the wood is cut long enough to fit in tightly, no fastening will be required, or at most a single band of wire near the top, embracing the whole column.

If the pillars or columns are white, wreaths of variegated or almost dead leaves should be used ; such will require no flowers, being sufficiently beautiful in themselves. Red and yellow shades should be employed in the centre of the wreaths, greener ones at top and bottom. If fern leaves are selected, they should be well soaked before being tied with the twine or wire.

Long wreaths of variegated forest leaves, Virginia

creeper, ivy, and hop-bine may be made on stout wire, and festooned from column to column, the whole length of the church, or they may be carried right across the nave, and perhaps midway may receive the support of a lamp standard ; if so, so much the better.   If no standards are in the centre, elegant bunches of flowers may be hung either in the centre of each garland or at intervals along it.   In place of flowers, bows of bright ribbon will be effective, especially if the ends are allowed to hang down for a foot or more.

Texts.

These should mostly be on a blue ground.   Blue serge looks as well as anything when it can be obtained in a pale shade.   The ordinary indigo dyed material will not do, as by artificial light it is to all intents perfectly black.   The letters may be formed of straw-plait of different widths, or of wheat-ears.   In the latter case, first cut out the letters in stout brown paper (that of a deep buff yellow is best), and paste or glue the ears of wheat on them.   Barley and rye are not so good for the purpose.

For a border round the inscription, barberries, black bryony, mountain ash, Virginia creeper, or single ivy leaves fastened on with $\frac{1}{4}$in. black tacks, may be used.   If necessary the capital letters may be formed of the red berries of the mountain ash, but for wheat letters capitals may be dispensed with, all of them being made of one height.

Another plan is to strain white serge upon the deal frame and to paste upon it the beautifully-coloured leaves of the Virginia creeper or the copper beech, and round the edge of the frame a row of green leaves of any kind.

With such a wealth of horticultural material to select from, it would seem a waste of colour and time to make illuminated texts ; they might be reserved for the dead season of the year—Christmas.   Suitable texts for harvest are given on the next page.

"The Bread of Life."

"Thou crownest the year with Thy goodness."

"He causeth the grass to grow for the cattle."

"In due season we shall reap, if we faint not."

"The earth is the Lord's, and the fulness thereof."

"O, all ye green things upon the earth, bless ye the Lord."

"Praise the Lord, O my soul, and forget not all His benefits."

"While the Earth remaineth, Seed-time and Harvest shall not cease."

"The Harvest is the End of the World, and the Reapers are the Angels."

"He maketh Peace in thy borders, and filleth thee with the finest of the wheat."

"Honour the Lord with thy Firstfruits; so shall thy Barns be filled with Plenty."*

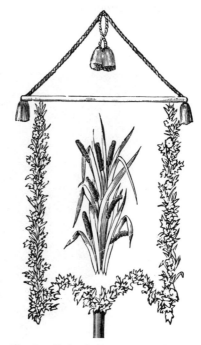

Fig. 87.—Bulrush Banner with border of Aquatic Flowers.

"Man doth not live by Bread only, but by every Word that proceedeth out of the Mouth of the Lord."

Banners and Shields.

A banner suitable for this festival is shown in Fig. 87. The background may be either red or blue, the latter for

---

* This text is very suitable for the chancel arch, being conveniently divided in the centre.

choice, and if it is of serge, the bulrushes may be sewn upon it.　If the ground is red, a wreath of green leaves interspersed with white aquatic flowers should be placed round it as a border; but if it is of blue, then fine variegated leaves of red, copper, and yellow should be stitched on.

Another banner may have a trophy of various kinds of corn as a centre-piece, and a border of moss around the outer edge.

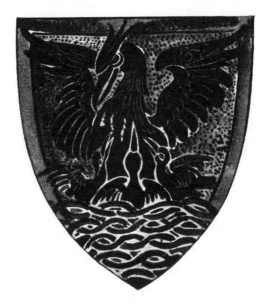

Fig. 88.—Shield showing the Pelican Feeding its Young, typifying Christ's Care and Providence.

Wheat surmounted by or thrust through the sacred monogram in scarlet flowers looks well, or a cross made of wheat bound with blue ribbon may be used, with little bouquets of flowers to fill up the corners.

Shields always look well, and in Figs. 88 to 90 are shown three suitable for this festival (for emblematic meaning see " Birds," in the paragraph under heading

" Emblems," on page 12). The examples given may be
carried out thus : Procure three pieces of thin zinc, 12in.
by 10in., and cut them to the shape shown. Paint them with
a coat of ordinary oil colour ; the tint is immaterial, as it is
only for a foundation. When quite dry rub smooth with a
piece of very fine sandpaper or used emery cloth. Sketch
out the device in pencil and gild the background. Then pro-

Fig. 89.—Shield showing the Phœnix Rising rom the Flames—the
Emblem of Seed rising from the Earth.

ceed to paint in the birds thus : Pelican brown, young birds a
grey-brown, the sticks forming nest a warm chocolate, and
the drops of blood red. For the Phœnix a warm grey should
be used, for the flames red and yellow, and for the nest
chocolate of a pale tone. The Peacock must be in its natural
colours and standing on a mound of green grass. When dry
bend the shields slightly convex, but on no account varnish

them, or the glints of crossing lights will render the devices difficult to discern at a short distance.

Small banners or shields bearing a device in leaves or flowers will be useful in many places in the church. If made from 8in. to 1ft. high they may be hung on the pew ends, or form centre-pieces for large floral devices or trellis work;

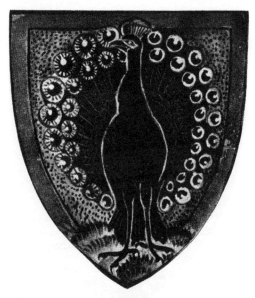

Fig. 90.—Shield showing the Peacock—the Emblem of Resurrection. The renewal of feathers typifies Harvest.

they may also find a place on the chancel-screen, but in that case should be made on a larger scale.

The Chancel-screen.

Where this exists, the main outlines may be followed by fastening narrow green wreaths, set with gay flowers, upon them; but where an ancient carved screen is not available, any carpenter will erect a skeleton one in a few hours, and paint or distemper it a dull green.

Harvest.

The outdoor vine, with bunches of white and purple grapes, has a handsome appearance on the screen, and looks very natural and realistic if the decoration is neatly executed. Hothouse vine leaves fade immediately, and should not be employed; hop-bine may be used instead.

Fig. 91.—Design for Hanging Screen between Nave and Chancel.

Virginia creeper, ivy, water lilies, bulrushes, gladioli, uva grass, palm leaves, and dried grasses also make up well. If water lilies, either white or yellow, are used, they should be thrust into hidden water tubes; the pure white comes out handsomely against the dark leaves of the foliage used.

In Fig. 91 is shown a charming device for a hanging

screen. The only wooden support required is a single deal batten fixed horizontally across the chancel opening, upon which may be placed a broad, straight wreath of leaves or evergreens of any kind. The perpendicular hanging wreaths are made up of corn with bunches of flowers and green leaves where shown. The festooned wreaths are made alternately of light and dark foliage, such as ivy, Passion flower leaves, Virginia creeper, ash twigs, clematis, hop-bine, or any other available foliage, and gladioli, dahlias of a pale colour, or scarlet geraniums may be arranged at intervals. Upon the wooden batten, above each trailing garland, a neatly made sheaf of corn should be placed, and the whole device hung with white and red shields charged with sacred emblems. Yellow ribbons should be used for the bows.

Fig. 92. — Door-way of Chancel-screen.

For a door-way, and to support the centre of the long batten, a framing consisting of two uprights and wire bent into cusps, as shown in Fig. 92, may be covered with ivy. This makes a very handsome and in-expensive screen, beneath which may repose a wealth of vegetables, fruits, and flowers, neatly disposed in baskets, wire stands, &c., and with plenty of feathery grass, fern, heather, &c., as accessories.

The Chancel.

The EAST WINDOW should be decorated according to the number of " lights " or panels it contains. If there are five separate window-sills, they may be each filled with moss or fern, bracken or heather, and from the centre sill should arise a great cross of wheat, barley, oats, and rye ; from those flanking it, two smaller ones made up of bulrushes, arrow-heads, water lilies, gladdon, and other riverside plants, tied with coloured ribbons, and from the two side windows smaller crosses of scarlet geraniums or other bright flowers.

The crosses must, of course, be commensurate with the size of the window, but for an ordinary church, 4ft. for the centre cross, 3ft. for the next two, and 2ft. for the outer ones will be suitable sizes.

If the sill extends across the whole window, some fine fruit may be exhibited on the green covering, such as melons, peaches, large apples, pineapples, grapes, &c., interspersed with berries of the mountain ash and any others at hand. From the centre of the sill, in this case, should rise a fine floral cross, such as Fig. 85, with sheaves of corn supporting it on either side, the end flowers being the largest red dahlias to be had, so as to make the ends of the cross into circular bosses.

Trellis work may cover the CHANCEL WALLS.

The COMMUNION RAILS may be entwined with clematis, hop-bine, or Virginia creeper, but nothing in the way of soft fruit should be used, as this may soil the cushions or the vestments of the officiating clergy. Flowers of any kind are permissible.

For the CHOIR STALLS, according to their shape, some little skill may be shown. A fine wreath of fruit, foliage, and flowers may be trailed in festoons along the front, tied here and there with coloured ribbons. Hard fruit may be strung on wire passed through it by means of a needle, and bunches of grapes may be suspended from ribbons. The ends of the stalls should be decked with trophies of river plants—white and yellow water lilies, bulrushes, sedges, and the purple-red heads of the reed. Above these may hang a banner or shield, and the whole may be capped with a crown of corn ears.

Pots of fine tall flowers may be ranged in front of the stalls, and should have a red background to show them up; in such case blue, yellow, and white flowers should be principally used, except where red flowers are tall enough to be well above the background.

The Communion Table.

The less this is adorned the better, as a fine frontal and its ordinary furniture require little in addition. A cross of lilies, or other white flowers, flanked by little sheaves of corn, made on a wire foundation into a resemblance to a fleur-de-lys is the only decoration that should be attempted. The upright wire may be trimmed with wheat, while the curving side wires may be garnished with barley and rye or oats, placed so that their heads hang gracefully downward. The centre may be bound with blue ribbon or a little garland of forget-me-nots.

If fruit *must* be included on the table, let it be restricted to apples and grapes, the former typifying the fall of man, and the latter Christ's atoning blood. These emblems should hang on either side of the centre cross upon a background of leaves—either autumn-tinted foliage or live green leaves, according to the colour of the background.

An illuminated text may grace the top edge of the frontal, if wished.

The Pulpit and Reading-desk.

The wreaths for both pulpit and reading-desk may be made of corn with the straw in three-plait, as being the easiest to make, the corn being put in thickly so that many ears may project from the plait, but where they are not sufficiently numerous others may be afterwards added. When the plait has been put in place, flowers and fine variegated leaves can easily be inserted between the straws without any other fastening.

The top wreaths of both pulpit and reading-desk are best of flowers, and the lower ones of fruit and berries. Among the latter are those of the laurel (*Aucuba*), which from their grape-like appearance have a fine decorative effect; so have the changing leaves and berries of the purple barberry, but they are difficult to obtain in many parts of England. The leaves of the copper beech are also very effective.

Elaborate designs and devices are in good taste for this festival, and many of those mentioned in these pages are suitable. Fig. 93 shows the Cross of Constantine, which may be built up, so far as the tall " P " is concerned, of leaves of golden laurel and dahlias, whilst the " X " may have a ground of oat straw fastened on in its round, uncrushed state. Upon this should be fastened a border of small flowers, with fine dahlias or other large blossoms at the four terminals.

Devices of flowers to fill side panels may be worked upon the grounds shown in Figs. 94 and 95. The first may be a white background and a red cross or the reverse; or the cross may be of red flowers on a bright green moss ground. The backgrounds of these panels, where several are required, may be worked in the colours appropriate to the season—red, blue, and yellow.

Palms—Kentia leaves from Howe Island in the Pacific, the great fan-like leaves of *Latania borbonica*, or the feathery ones of *Areca lutescens*—will all aid in giving that peculiar, hazy, mystic effect that is so beautiful.

Fig. 93.—Cross of Constantine in Laurel, Oat-straw, Dahlias, &c.

For the front panel of the pulpit a cross of white lilies on a red or yellow-green background is charming.

A device of berries upon a neat banner may hang from the reading-desk. It may be a device of the Trinity, or really of any kind except those for Christmas or the Passion Week, as God's bounty continues the whole year round.

The Font.

This should not have corn upon it, as that is so much used in other parts of the church. Nor need it have any emblems of autumn. An abundance of white flowers should be used, mingled with blush roses, pink geraniums, lobelias, forget-me-nots, and others of delicate colouring, and the wreaths upon which they are placed should be of the palest and handsomest kinds. Bright glaring colours are always out of place on a font, which in itself is an emblem of innocence and purity, and quite out of harmony with primary, full, and

Figs. 94 and 95.—Simple Devices for filling in Pulpit-panels.

bold colouring. For this reason many object to place fruit with its broad glow of colours around the font base, but where such is a universal feature, it is of little avail to write against it. A too lavish display need not, however, be made, and the rich colours of the fruit may be toned down by the use of grey moss, grey leaves, and the grey buff of dried palms and foreign leaves. The use of bulrushes and

Fig. 96.—Wire Foundation for Wreath encircling Font.

water lilies, typical of water, will also aid in quieting any tendency to garish colouring. A wreath may be made upon a wire foundation as in Fig. 96, which may then be bent round the body of the font and fastened.

Where the decorations are to remain for several days, it is best either to have a simple device floating upon the water ; or, if the font cover is retained, so to build up the decoration that the whole may be removed bodily. This precaution is necessary when the font has to be used for baptism.

Remember that if cut flowers are stuck into a large potato it will preserve them for a considerable time, and that a little camphor or charcoal placed in the water in which flowers are stood will also add to their life. Wet sand, sawdust, moss, and cotton-wool placed in flower troughs are also preservatives.

The Porch.

It is usual to place fine tall sheaves of corn on either side of the porch. These look well if cross-garnished with broad blue ribbons and a wreath of bright red flowers is garlanded round them. A festoon of flowers may also hang above the entrance door, and such a text of welcome as the following may be worked in wheat-ears on a pale blue ground : " I will offer in His tabernacle sacrifices of joy."

The Entrance-gateway.

This may have an arch of flowers over it—just a heavy green wreath with flowers placed high upon it, so as to be out of reach of busy little hands. A device so placed proclaims to passers-by that they are free to enter and give thanks, though they may not be habitual worshippers at the church. " Come into His Courts " is a suitable text.

In conclusion it may be remarked that the aim of this little work has been to point out the appropriate emblems for the various festivals, to particularise the many materials used in the making-up of the various decorations and devices, and to show how, with taste and forethought, and at a small cost, a church may be garnished in a pleasing and correct manner.

It should be remembered that *decoration* means the beautifying of a church or other sacred building for a specific occasion, not cumbering it with an overwhelming mass of

L

foliage and inartistic piles of fruit, with the idea that the greater the amount of material used, the finer and more elegant the effect. A few neatly-made and well-placed garlands, embellished with a sprinkling of flowers, are much more likely to please the eye than a whole cartload of evergreens formed into cumbrous wreaths and hung in inartistic disarray. Provided that the general idea of the whole scheme of decoration is simple, the colours employed few, the fruit and flowers placed gemlike in a green setting, and the banners, shields, and devices exhibited in prominent and telling positions, the whole effect will be æsthetic and pleasing. Everything should be under the direction of one or two experienced persons, and all the work carried out in a cleanly, methodical, and reverent manner, remembering that noise, laughter, and levity are out of keeping with the sacred character of the building to be decorated, and that the whole work is not for the glory of the individual decorator, but to the praise and glory of God—the Giver of all good things.

INDEX.

Standard Works.

Old English Churches.

By GEO. CLINCH, F.G.S. Magnificently Illustrated. In cloth gilt, price 6/6 nett, bypost 6/10.

English Antiquities,

With a concise Dictionary ot Terms, &c., used. By GEORGE CLINCH, F.G.S. Well Illustrated. In cloth, price 6/6 nett, by post 6/10.

Decorative Painting

And Etching upon Various Materials. By B. C. SAWARD. In cloth gilt, price 3/6 nett, by post 3/10.

London :
L. Upcott Gill, Bazaar Buildings, Drury Lane, W.C.

INDEX.

L. UPCOTT GILL, LONDON & COUNTY PRINTING WORKS, DRURY LANE, W.C.